WOODSTOCK

A Story of Middle Americans

By Bill Tammeus

AuthorHouse™ LLC
1663 Liberty Drive
Bloomington, IN 47403
www.authorhouse.com
Phone: 1-800-839-8640

Published by AuthorHouse 02/06/2014

ISBN: 978-1-4918-5602-4 (sc)
*   978-1-4918-5603-1 (e)*

Library of Congress Control Number: 2014901529

Any people depicted in stock imagery provided by Thinkstock are models,
and such images are being used for illustrative purposes only.
Certain stock imagery © Thinkstock.

This book is printed on acid-free paper.

authorHOUSE®

WOODSTOCK

A Story of Middle Americans

By Bill Tammeus

Table of Contents

Introduction

THE TOWER OF THE OPERA HOUSE LOOKS OUT OVER THE SQUARE IN WOODSTOCK, ILLINOIS.

The deep roots of something essential, something that helped to inform and define the soul of contemporary America, can be found in the middle of the Twentieth Century and in the middle of the country. A generation — my generation and some who came soon before and after us — grew up with values, outlooks, approaches, commitments, experiences, relationships and, maybe most important, adaptation abilities that would shape the country for the next 70 years and no doubt more.

It has taken me most of those seven decades to begin to understand all of this. And just when I'm sure I've got it about right I tell myself to keep looking because surely there's more to uncover. And there is. But now it's important to me to write down what I think I know about this era and why it matters to anyone else. So my immodest hope is that in this small book you will find enlightenment, insight and perhaps even wisdom about the influences that helped to form today's America — for both good and ill. If you are searching for all the reasons America is what it is today, I can't offer an exhaustive explanation. No one can. But I can point to a few important pieces of such an explanation.

When you get through, I hope you will find that I have mostly avoided what regularly ticked off one of my favorite authors, Kurt Vonnegut Jr., who in a 1978 letter to his publisher wrote this:

"I am tired of people who examine their pasts and find nothing but mortal woundings."[1] Most of my mortal woundings came well after the middle of the Twentieth Century. I won't claim that growing up in Woodstock, Illinois, starting in 1945 was the equivalent of living trouble free in paradise. It wasn't. But eventually I learned to read between the societal lines, to dissect the cultural frogs hopping about all around me so I could begin to see what they were made of, to extract from my experiences lessons that would serve me well as I moved into and through adulthood. And what was true of me was true of many — maybe most — of my contemporaries, whom I will call Middle Americans.

I'll share some of that to help you see how my personal journey was in many ways a uniquely American experience with, if not universal, at least widespread resonance for the rest of the country. What I encountered and processed became, given world enough and time, quintessentially American ways of doing life that have shaped our nation in countless ways into its current state, forming it in the immediate wake of what now is regularly called the "greatest generation." (A problematic term, but let it go.)

When I use the phrase Middle America or the middle of the country, I mean more than geography, though clearly my hometown northwest of Chicago could be said to be quite roughly equidistant from the East and West coasts, to say nothing of being south of Canada and north of Mexico. And at 954 feet above sea level (a level recorded on the old McHenry County Courthouse on The Square in Woodstock) it also occupies a middle ground of elevation. So, yes, it was in the middle, give or take a few hundred miles horizontally and a few hundred or maybe thousand feet vertically.

But Middle America stretches geographically beyond the Midwest. It was and is, finally, a state of mind, a middle-class way of living that has more to do with industriousness than with wealth, more to do with an eagerness to learn than with advanced college degrees, more with an openness to possibilities than with the benefits of inheritance, with an ability to know we need to adapt and change than with a resolute determination to remain fixed in place. It has to do with a capacity for outrage when, finally, we have seen enough. It also has to do with being pragmatic, practical, optimistic, ethical, problem-solving, patriotic in a broad sense and not cynical. We were and are more open-hearted than open-minded, but at our best we are both.

You could be, in other words, a Middle American while living in Eugene, Oregon, or Sarasota, Florida, or Rochester, New York. But in Woodstock, Illinois, it was hard *not* to be a Middle American in the middle of the Twentieth Century. Which is to say that it was hard not to be rooted in the importance of trustworthiness, of family strength even when families were disintegrating, of gratitude for the chance to live in a fabulous country that was, of course, sometimes deeply flawed. Yes, for many people there was an insularity to living in Middle America, a blocked vision (think of Richard Nixon's morally pinched Silent Majority, egged on by that nincompoop Spiro T. Agnew), a self-satisfaction that could be infuriating, especially to people who had traveled the world and widened their vision. But in the end we knew we could rely on one another and could be free enough to imagine new answers, new methods for staying on the bucking bronco of life. We could even imagine new futures.

So if we didn't personally invent fax machines, cell phones, personal computers, high-definition televisions, social media tools, jet airplanes, hybrid cars, TV dinners, wrinkle-free shirts or the Moog synthesizer, we were willing to see how all that and more might fit into our lives. And when I say more, I include an embrace of people who discover they are gay. I include people who are adherents of religions different from ours. And I include people who were not, like so many of us, white Protestants with European roots.

Beyond all of that, for those of us who grew up in Woodstock, our civil, simple, clear-eyed Midwestern ways benefited from being in a place that, as author and essayist Thomas Frank wrote about nearby Chicago, "set your bullshit detector on hair trigger, permanently; it allowed you to see right through the fatuity of the moment. The healthiness of this is, I think, impossible to deny, especially when you look back over the long parade of delusions that have in the intervening years gripped the nation's leadership class, eroding our politics, journalism, economy, and institutions of higher ed."[2] (For more about this "long parade of delusions," see my later chapter on institutional failures.)

We may not have been "the greatest generation" and we may not have been the first to have adapted to swift change, but our steady, count-the-cards ways of meeting the future ultimately meant we could integrate these changes into our lives without dissolving into revolution, violence or social insanity. Being from a town that for decades produced manual Woodstock and Oliver typewriters, I may have been reluctant to switch to IBM Selectrics and then to computer keyboards. After all, we Woodstock folks had skin in the game. But eventually we and other Middle Americans recognized the inevitable — in this and in so many other matters.

It may sound as if I'm giving us Middle Americans way too much credit, but the truth is that we modeled how to live wisely, sanely, even mindfully. If certain segments of the nation now are throwing off all that was and is good about Middle America — as now it sometimes appears to be the case, with the worst of the Tea Party members being Exhibit A — such an abandonment is a political, social and cultural miscalculation of the worst sort. Middle Americans are not, in the end, ideologues, not fundamentalists of any sort, not people bloated with false certitude who know all the answers even before they hear the questions, not people willing to shut down the government out of spite.

We are, rather, the essentially healthy products of a flawed time. We sometimes could see the flaws and eventually even think aloud about ways to fix them. No, we didn't get everything right. Not at all. Indeed, our children, grandchildren and great-grandchildren may well have good reasons to shake their heads at us because of the stupid wars we started or (more accurately) fought in, the selfish ways we wounded the planet environmentally while burdening generations to come with the enormous debt of a fiscally careless nation.

And yet I contend that there was and is a certain core decency about Middle Americans that set the tone for what was good and noble and generous and touching about the nation — even when some of that nation's policies were battering Middle Americans and pretty much the whole middle class while offering the very wealthy all kinds of unnecessary breaks and subsidies. I personally fail each day at being good and noble and generous and touching, but to the extent I succeed, I can trace the roots of that to growing up in a good family in Woodstock, Illinois, an imperfect town in an imperfect state in an imperfect country filled with imperfect people who sometimes could take your breath away with their goodness, nobility, generosity and heart. I hope the stories I tell here will help you see what I mean and that you will want to honor such characteristics.

In my collection of Woodstock memorabilia I have the Student Handbook from what I believe is my freshman (1959-'60) year at Woodstock Community High School. That handbook is telling in at least two ways. First, its cover demonstrates the semi-serious teen-age silliness of the time. By which I mean that with a light blue pen I once edited the word "Community" on that cover to read "Communist." Nice.

But second, and more to the point, the booklet opens with the "School Code." I reproduce it here because in many ways we Middle Americans marinated in such codes and they never left our DNA.

I, a student of Woodstock Community High School, in order to develop a foundation for better citizenship, desire to promote and encourage habits and ideals that will lead to the development of good character and the attachment of the highest moral values in every day living.

By accepting and practicing the following principles, I believe I will be a better citizen and will insure a better future for myself, my school, and my nation.

1. **I will judge people by their merits regardless of race, religion, or nationality.**
2. **I will maintain honesty in my relations with others.**
3. **I will strive to attain high standards of cleanliness of person, thought, and behavior.**
4. **I will realize my responsibilities to the school and the groups of which I am a part.**
5. **I will consider the interests and convictions of my fellow men equally with my own.**
6. **I will be mindful of my own promises and responsible for my own actions.**
7. **I will respect personal and public property.**
8. **I will display sportsmanship as a participant or spectator in school functions.**
9. **I will observe the rules of safety at all times.**
10. **I will abstain from smoking or the use of profanity in school or where it might reflect upon the school.**

I am not claiming that we always and everywhere have abided by the values expressed in this or similar codes, but it contains a message about values that we eventually internalized. And such values have helped to create us as Middle Americans, who in turn helped to create what the nation is today for better or worse. And I contend it's mostly for better.

The Square

◄———————►

IN WOODSTOCK'S CENTER IS THE SQUARE, WITH ITS FOCUS ON HISTORY AND PATRIOTISM.

"Wanna scoop the loop one more time?" — The inevitable question asked by whichever of us teenagers was driving others around and around The Square on an evening, looking for, well, whatever we were looking for.

Despite assurances from parents and preachers, coaches and teachers that virtue in my hometown was ubiquitous, there was always a hint of darkness at the edges of our young lives, always a disquieting suspicion that the mother of boys our age had committed suicide for an understandable reason, always a hunch that people who shouldn't have been were, nonetheless, having sex, getting drunk, cheating on their taxes and not closing their eyes when they prayed.

That foreboding, whether justified or not, was part of the reason that The Square in Woodstock was, in the end, our organizing principle, our home plate, our tether-ball pole. It was at once a geographical, spiritual and social center but also — in a controlled, careful sort of way — serendipitously generous to us. It always gave us a place to call home (however uneasy we were there), a center of gravity that provided the boundaries inside of which we could try to resolve the terrible, but often unarticulated, ambiguities of life in the middle of the century, in the middle of the country, in the middle of The American Dream, which was — even if we wished to deny it — part nightmare. It was this sense of stability — uneasy, to be sure, but stable nonetheless — that most characterized Middle America.

It was either to forget our fears or perhaps to live into them that we came to The Square and drove around and around and around it when we were teen-agers. The relentless circles — for we rounded the corners of The Square's streets into circles in our borrowed cars — gave us constancy, gave us pattern, gave us dependable structure and, in that sense, helped to make us the kind of people I call Middle Americans. We were looking for something as we circled The Square, but probably none of us could have said exactly what. So it is only decades later that I now recognize what I found there.

The Square, laid out in 1844, consists of four short streets of equal length — West Van Buren, South Benton, Cass and North Johnson — that surround a lovely little park that could have come from Norman Rockwell's paint brushes. In the 1950s and '60s it had — and still has today — a covered bandstand, an eventually rebuilt spring house (the original lasted from 1873 into the 1930s), benches, a soldiers' monument ("Erected to the Soldiers 1861-65"), a drinking fountain, crisscrossing sidewalks, grass (in season), trees and people who actually use the park as a place of respite and a place to be seen even as they come to watch others.

The Square was and is an ordered Midwestern version of the elongated, slightly irregular village green of Woodstock, Vermont, after which my Woodstock was named because some of its important early settlers came from that small New England town. If you've seen the movie "Groundhog Day," you've seen The Square. Woodstock dressed up as Punxsutawney, Pennsylvania, for that movie and much of the movie takes place in or around The Square. It's a darn good movie, but it's hard for people from Woodstock to watch it for the story instead of for all the places they recognize.

The Square pulled on us the way black holes are said to draw on the space around them. The difference was that — unlike light from black holes — many of us emerged from The Square physically, even as, finally, The Square helped to create in us a radical sense of order, a routine, a pattern that we have never fully thrown over, and now don't wish to.

The Square was working on us in that way in the very center of town while, at the edges of Woodstock, the rich northern Illinois farmland reinforced that sense of order with row after straight row of corn or soybeans. As we'd pass by these rows in our cars — or even, earlier, on our bicycles — they planted in us an appreciation for the necessity of order. We Middle Americans are not compulsive about order, not obsessive. But eventually we prefer order over chaos, organization over randomness.

Each of the long and impressive rows of corn and soybeans was spaced equidistant from a row that was — for all that most passing eyes could tell — identical to it. The farmers who planted such rows — my grandfathers among them, though farther south in Illinois — understood the economic benefits of precise field geometry. They planted efficiently, with order in mind, and harvested the same way.

From early summer through harvest each year when I was a boy, I would pass these rows — agriculture's rhythmic patterns, its lines and angles, its tacks and turns, its repetitious calculus, its sensible drillings and expectant hopings. And all this necessary order, this important preference for one-then-two-then-three has imprinted itself on me and many other Middle Americans in almost a genetic way, sculpting us quite irrevocably.

In some ways, I and the people I grew up with have spent our lives since then testing new ways of doing and seeing things to determine if the order stamped on us as children is still useful or, instead, is blocking us from becoming whole and liberated people. Sometimes our efforts have been stumbling, sometimes anarchistic, sometimes uncomprehending.

I cannot speak for all Middle Americans or even all of my generation from Woodstock, but I have been well served by the order I found in both The Square at the center and the crop rows at the edges of Woodstock. Often I have strained under the insistent demands of this order, its careful nose-counting ways, its everything-in-its-place requirements, its locked, stocked and barreled determination. And sometimes I have become untethered from this order in dangerous ways. But it has marked me indelibly, and I often return to The Square and the farmland — in thought if not in person — to honor them and give thanks for helping to create the banks of the river that I am and that other Middle Americans are as well.

832 Dean Street

WHEN I LIVED IN THIS HOUSE AS A BOY A CONVENIENCE STORE WAS ATTACHED ON THE RIGHT, NOT THAT OTHER HOUSE.

Although I've often seen a photo, reproduced here, that froze the moment, my first memory is not of me sitting on top of an upright piano in my first home at 832 Dean Street — Christmas 1947, I would say (incorrectly, it turns out, despite my memory of it being at 832 Dean because my sister Mary is in the shot and she wasn't born until after we moved from the 832 house, so it must be Christmas 1948).

Nor is my first memory of the time I cut my right thumb on a tin can near the back door of that house. You still can see that fat bowl-shaped scar today, but I don't recall the accident.

Rather, my first memory is of a toy box on the enclosed front porch of 832 Dean and, one snowy day, a woman and little girl my age knocking on the door of the porch to visit my mother. It's an essentially meaningless

memory. Why that woman? Why her daughter (who later would be my classmate)? Why the snow? What peculiar thing caused that — and not something else — to lodge in my brain as a first memory? I simply don't know. I know only that the rippled storehouses of the mind are nearly incomprehensible — and that they help to make us who we are. They also use the memories stored in them to help give us an understanding of what home means. And if we Middle Americans know anything, it's what home means.

The house at 832 Dean Street always will feel something like home to me. By contrast, several other places where I've lived never have felt like home and doubtless never will. It's odd. Even if we have moved dozens of times, pinballing around the world, only certain places are home.

Each time I come back to Woodstock now I drive by the small, oddly shaped house on a wedge-corner lot where my family lived when I was born. The house has changed in more recent years, especially with the removal of the tiny grocery, or convenience, store that was attached to it. By age three, I was living several blocks away in the house that would remain in my family for nearly fifty years. But it was at 832 Dean, a house with not only an attached convenience store but also with a neighborhood park — Sunnyside — just across the street, where I locked in that earliest memory.

I WAS A HAPPY TODDLER AT 832 DEAN STREET, THOUGH I LET MY DIAPER SHOW INDISCREETLY.

The late author Kurt Vonnegut once wrote that when he drives into his hometown of Indianapolis, this question haunts him: Where's my bed? I know what he means. Sometimes I drive by 832 Dean Street and wonder if whoever lives there now would let me sleep the innocent sleep of infancy there again — a sleep my conscious mind cannot remember, though surely the memory is in there somewhere and might be excavated by some psychiatrist, hypnotist or witch doctor.

This house is not, of course, the only place that draws me to it by a homing call. So I am moved to ask: What is it that leads us to find home in some locations but not in others? What causes us to understand at some visceral level that we belong here or there but not, say, somewhere else? And what has caused Middle Americans generally to feel at home and comfortable in this giant, pasted-together land, parts of which some of us have never seen? (As I write this, there still are three states I've never been in — Montana, Idaho and Alaska.)

I have come to believe that home is where we are free to be our whole selves. That is, we feel at home in those places where we are liberated to be authentically who, at our essence, we are, with as few masks as possible.

I almost never felt that sense of wholeness in the Woodstock house in which I grew up at 415 West South Street. For many reasons, my mother seemed unwilling to release control of my three sisters and me so we could discover and live out our destinies. Each of us had to do that in different ways and to greater or lesser extents without Mom's help or permission, and do it away from the home in which we spent most of our childhoods.

That may explain why my sisters and I have lived most of our adult lives scattered almost literally from coast to coast — from California to North Carolina — with just one of us within fifty miles of that house, the sister who felt most comfortable in the West South Street home.

And yet there is something about that house that feels like home to me. I think it's because I now understand that it was there that I first came to terms with the reality that I was not free, and it was there that I purposed to be free some day. So I am drawn to that place because it remains the site of my liberating decision to find home somewhere. Some Middle Americans, of course, almost always feel comfortable in the homes of their origin while others must struggle to locate that comfort. But eventually most of us have found it.

Home, then, is not always a place free of pain or anxiety. Rather, it is where distress has been confronted and, in some way, resolved — or at least understood.

The house in which my children grew up will always feel like home to me, too, even though, as my marriage to their mother dissolved in the early and mid-1990s, it was the nexus of scalding anxiety and unwholesome discord as we struggled with the affair she chose to have. But despite that, the house was also where we reared two beautiful, healthy daughters who brought — and still bring — both of us joy.

I can think of places I've lived, however, that feel nothing like home to me today. One was the dormitory of a boarding school in India where I spent part of my twelfth year. For countless reasons, other children did not accept me there, and I felt like an unwanted alien in a strange land. In fact, for a time that's exactly what I was.

I have come to understand now much of what that was about, and I don't doubt that I could return to that school and that dorm today without bitterness just as I have come to know and enjoy as adults some of the children who were in that school with me then. Still, I'm sure that the old dorm will never feel like home.

Similarly, there's a small studio apartment in Rochester, New York, that I occupied for about a year starting in mid-1967. It was my first post-college dwelling place. But even from the beginning it felt like a temporary roost to me, a nest some other bird had built and in which I was trespassing. Nothing about it felt like the permanence of home.

By contrast, Ghost Ranch, a national Presbyterian conference center where I teach and where the artist Georgia O'Keeffe lived and painted in northern New Mexico, feels like home to me even though I have been just a temporary resident there each summer for only a week. And yet because I am free at the ranch to be myself — and to uncover some parts of that self that get neglected in the busyness of most of the rest of my year — I am quite at home there.

Many people have tried to describe what home really is, perhaps most famously the poet Robert Frost, who said: "Home is the place where, when you have to go there, / They have to take you in." And nearly two thousand years ago, Pliny the Elder offered this: "Home is where the heart is," a phrase that no doubt became a cliché within a week of its first utterance.

I now know that Frost's observation isn't always true and that Pliny needs editing. I would put it this way: Home is where the healed heart — this side of heaven — is most free. And, in the end, one reason that we Middle Americans have had confidence about our lives is because, most of the time — almost no matter where we are — we feel at home.

415 West South Street

THE HOUSE AS IT LOOKS TODAY.

At the bottom of the hill behind our big-boned, resolute house, on the way to the orchard and garden, the mortal remains of an ancient pump for a water well somehow survived year after year. The thing never worked when we lived there but the square wooden base and the rusty metal machinery rising out of it stood ready to be kicked back into service. Or at least I imagined so.

It was, in fact, that corpse of a well in that hilly yard that helped to form my imagination and to remind me almost daily that I was connected to history, even if I did not know the details of that history. So, like some of our politicians today, I would make up history. I would pretend that long ago someone had fallen into the well and drowned. Some days the drowned person was a helpless toddler. Other times I thought of the victim as a teen-age suicide. Each time I passed the well, in fact, the person who drowned changed.

13

Drowning there was not so crazy an idea. Those things happen. For instance, when one of my brothers-in-law was in high school, his father fell into a silo on his farm at the edge of Woodstock and died. Besides, the possibly apocryphal story about our property, which measured nearly an acre, was that it once

had been a cemetery — perhaps for Native American residents of the area, perhaps for early white settlers before the town was incorporated. The stories differed. So death seemed somehow at home there, somehow a familiar tenant. And because death often is not welcome anywhere in death-denying America, it must find a home where it can.

MY FAMILY IN THE HOUSE ABOUT 1953.

My imaginings about the well were part of a pattern. The whole property at 415 West South Street seemed to encourage lively imaginings. Without a place where the imagination is free to explore, childhood would be short-circuited, diminished, nearly wasted. Henry Ward Beecher had it right: "The soul without imagination is what an observatory would be without a telescope."[3]

Almost every place in that house and on those grounds seemed to call forth the wild imaginings of children, and maybe even adults. So even as the real future was rushing at us Middle Americans with sometimes-terrifying speed, we also could imagine various potential futures — some lively, some quite moribund. When I was in college, I wrote a poem about the old Civil War colonel, William Avery, who built 415 West South Street for his family in 1883. I imagined that somehow he had died in the attic (accessible only through a narrow ceiling opening in one of the upstairs bedrooms) and that no one knew it until someone came across the colonel's brittle bones decades later. In part of that poem, I imagined this:

> *Poor old bastard.*
> *His corroded cranium was probably*
> *once filled with porcelain dreams,*
> *compartments, categories,*
> *where now only dust lies and*
> *a curious spider crawls and*
> *spins its silken trap to catch*
> *the fly that has landed on the*
> *colonel's long chin.*

It was, of course, a poem reflecting the maturity and writing skills of a college student, but it offers, I think, a little insight into the idea that we rely on imagination to help us understand reality. And, as I say, the house and grounds of 415 West South Street provided for me the geography and opportunity to see where imagination might take me. Without imagination, would we today have an Internet (thanks, Al Gore), computers, sophisticated medicines for complex diseases, polyester, drones, iPad apps?

In my imagination, as I would race down the back hill, over or through a fence, between neighbors' houses and up to the playground of Dean Street School on a summer's morning, I could see the day when

I would turn in the scruffy old baseball mitt I was carrying for a real Major League glove so I could play third base for the Chicago Cubs — who, God knows, could use all the help they can get — then and now.

Sometimes I would sit on a flat part of the roof of 415, which could be reached only through a hatch door in the upstairs storeroom, and look out over the trees in the orchard, imagining all sorts of things: That I could fly by leaping off the roof; that I could hide up there forever — or at least until I finished reading all the books I wanted to read; that some day God would quit hiding from me and speak clearly.

At night in my bedroom, which faced the street at the front of our house, I would watch as the lights from passing cars sent shadowed window shapes around and around my walls, and I would imagine who was in those cars. There were lovers on their way to some secluded parking spot, frustrated old men running away from angry old women, night workers on their way to conduct trains on the Chicago & Northwestern commuter line that ran through Woodstock, nurses and doctors headed just up the street to the hospital, there to patch together people whose bodies were somehow spinning apart.

The Twentieth Century Swiss psychiatrist and psychotherapist Carl Jung, who had several good ideas in his career, was absolutely right when he wrote that "without playing with. . .fantasy no creative work has ever come to birth. The debt we owe to the play of imagination is incalculable."[4]

Jung may not have had my childhood home and yard in mind and the way it encouraged me to play with fantasy, to imagine, to dream — or the homes and yards of other Middle Americans finding their own sources of imagination — but it's hard to conceive what our lives would have become without those sources. And it's hard to imagine how anyone can construct a healthy life without the space and time to let our minds run freely into anarchistic streets.

So when I ask God to preserve us from life without metaphor, I think about that segment of our population that needs everything in black and white, up and down. I think about the biblical literalists, the legalists and fundamentalists of all stripe. And I feel a deep sadness that, unlike many Middle Americans, they seem to have grown up without a playground for the imagination.

Hideouts

SOME OF THE BOYS WHO JOINED OUR HIDEOUT GROUP ATTENDED BOB OKESON'S TENTH BIRTHDAY PARTY IN 1955. I'M NEXT TO THE GIRL SIPPING FROM HER GLASS. THAT'S BOB ON THE FAR LEFT WITH HIS MOUTH OPEN.

Behind the big yellow house in which Cora White slept when she wasn't at Dean Street School a few blocks away teaching us second graders, a row of tall bushes hid a small drop-off in the back yard.

We slipped behind those bushes — two or three other boys and I — and created our first hideout, an invisible space between the branches and the sloping land where we could breathe freedom and avoid the demands of a world that seemed simply to order second-graders around as if they were chess pieces.

As we approached our safe place, we would look up and down Putnam Avenue, paying special attention to the high school across the street to make sure that no one saw us disappear into the bushes from the sidewalk. Apparently we weren't careful enough. One day not long after we located this spot, some adult — possibly at the urging of Miss White herself, though I've always blamed my mother — stopped us from entering our hideout and made up a rule that said it was forevermore off limits.

This was not, however, the last place we hid, our last attempt at privacy, at self-exile from family and responsibility. The basement of First Presbyterian Church and its dark corners behind the furnace served later (more about that in a later chapter). And the tree house we built in the Okeson family's back yard just up the street from my house — a rough but complex two-story wooden affair — was our hideout one junior-high summer. We hid girlie magazines and cigarettes there until Mr. Okeson found us out and ordered the mansion deconstructed.

All these years later, I still think about why — and from what — we were hiding. And what I have decided is that we created our own spaces because we knew instinctively — without any ability to articulate it — that we needed a place to try out being our true selves. To do this, we had to be where none of the insistent distractions of parental and community discipline could be found — although for most Middle Americans those distractions, as we thought of them, were pretty much constant and almost always constructive in nature. Our rivers needed a place to spill over their banks now and again, to create small channels of experiment, to meander and to fall down steep and rocky beds. Thank goodness lots of Middle Americans had such places to sort out who they were.

I suppose it might have been possible to extend this yearning for a separate world into something strange and even malevolent. *The Lord of the Flies*[5] may be fiction, but it speaks a profound truth about our fathomless capacity for — and attraction to — evil.

The families watching over us, however, generally were attentive as well as being safe and loving havens from other storms. So although we pushed against boundaries and did a few things we never wanted to confess to our parents, on the whole it was innocent searching for limits, for the edges of our consciences.

And yet the motivation to create hideouts is both healthy and potentially destructive. We learned in some of our later hideouts to gaze upon the female body with lust and to encourage lust in each other. We males learned to value women for their looks first — and it wouldn't surprise me to learn that girls in their hideouts were thinking about boys in a meat-market sort of way, too. (I say this from having grown up with three sisters.) The attitude we boys learned has caused enormous damage not only to the exploited women but to the men who never mature beyond that. There is some animal instinct in all of us that drives us toward sex, but if we do not find ways to value sex as one of God's healthful gifts, we simply use others and they become commodities. And yet using others was what we began to learn about in our hideouts. We had to learn respect for sex elsewhere and later.

But there were good things, too. There was the trust we learned to put in each other. We trusted each other not to give our hideouts away, not to invite others in without unanimous consent, not to push us toward evil so hard that we could not resist. We learned the value of good company, of laughter not shared with adults, of the freedom to ask hard questions and offer unorthodox answers about eternal matters — answers that might have set on edge the teeth of our parents, teachers and preachers.

I came to value time alone — those instances when I was the first into or last out of the hideout. I still cherish such time and find that my internal compass runs amok when I don't have enough of it. It also runs amok if that's all I have. So I learned to value the balance of time alone and time in the company of others. And I think most Middle Americans found that balance, too. At least that's a common response when it comes up in conversation.

I never knew exactly where my own children found their hideouts. And I'm glad I didn't. But they have become whole and healthy adults, so I must assume they learned where to find them and how to use them. And as they now have children of their own, I hope my daughters, too, will give their youngsters the freedom to slip away and find their own space behind the home of some new Miss White so the wholesome values of such places can create yet more Middle Americans.

The Rebel

THIS FRONT SECTION OF DEAN STREET SCHOOL HAS NOT CHANGED FROM THE TIME I STARTED KINDERGARTEN THERE IN 1950.

My life of radical rebellion against authority began — and ended — the first day I entered kindergarten at Dean Street School in 1950.

On that clear September morning, my mother handed me over to the unsought embrace of teacher Lila Dobbs, who tried to convince me that I would have a wonderful time in the class, especially if first I were to join Melodee Church playing in the sandbox. But I wanted nothing to do with Mrs. Dobbs, the sand, Melodee or anything else connected with this manipulative enterprise. In fact, all I wanted to do was to go home.

Which is what I did.

When Mrs. Dobbs wasn't looking, I slipped out the door, up the one flight of stairs leading to ground level, out one of the heavy doors of the "GIRLS' ENTRANCE" (yes, all caps) and into a school yard — only partly fenced — filled with older children who were at recess or who, perhaps, hadn't yet started class.

A girl there — I think she knew who I was — asked what I thought I was doing as a kindergartner out there.

"Going home," I said.

She started to protest, but before she could locate words of astonishment and discipline, I was past her and on the way to my house three or so blocks away. For some reason she didn't try to stop me.

When I arrived, I opened the back door into the kitchen and — not finding my mother there — went upstairs, where I located her lying down for a nap.

"I'm home," I announced. "I'm not going to school anymore."

I don't remember seeing my mother move so quickly and with such determination before or since. In about thirteen seconds, she had delivered me for a second time to Mrs. Dobbs, who, embarrassed by my escape, promised my mother that I would not be leaving unnoticed again.

And I didn't. In fact, I soon learned that Mrs. Dobbs wanted my presence each morning much more than did my mother. And, better, Mrs. Dobbs thought I was perhaps the finest, most well-behaved child ever to go through kindergarten. When, for instance, Roger Knuth, may he rest in peace, would act out, Mrs. Dobbs would ask him, "Why can't you sit quietly like Billy Tammeus?" I both hated it and loved it.

In this way, I learned how to please authority figures — but never in a sycophantish sort of way. That is, I knew what they wanted and usually gave it to them, all the while recognizing that they seemed to need getting it more than I needed to give it to them. I was not a devoted member of their cults. I maintained emotional distance. I withheld my adoration and I somehow understood that people of authority could abuse their power out of egotistical need or misuse it out of good-hearted incompetence. So my devotion was always conditional, tentative — so far as it was possible for a five-year-old to adopt such a stance. And that's also the way it has been for me as an adult. I think, in fact, that it is the most healthful way to survive — except in a marriage or with your family.

It was, in part, this detached attitude among the people of my generation I call Middle Americans that helped to create the soil in which the authority-rejecting 1960s could grow. Even then I was no rebel, no hippie, no druggie, no dropout. And most Middle Americans weren't, either. I was detached even from radical detachment. But I lived skeptically, cautiously, never quite trusting people in power, always suspecting that, like Mrs. Dobbs, they wanted my devotion but were, in the end, unworthy of it because they were flawed — and so, in fact, was I. My own flawed nature was one reason I was unwilling to declare my unconditional allegiance to almost any cause. I recognized that I might be wrong, might have misjudged something, might have run across a person of authority who needed me to behave more than I needed to offer such behavior.

The world seems to have an abundance of people whom Eric Hoffer, in the title of his book, labeled "True Believers,"[6] which is to say people who give themselves unreservedly to some cause even if that cause deserves only tentative support. Religious fanatics are especially distressing and destructive, but they are far from the only people who have not learned to withhold complete allegiance to some flawed institutions, persons or ideas or who regularly vote against their own self-interest.

I wish I could tell you what it was about Mrs. Dobbs that made me reluctant to give her my unbridled obedience. Maybe it was what, on that first day, I judged to be her cloying enthusiasm. Or maybe it was her occasionally odd language. The coats we wore on chilly days, for instance, were not coats to her but "wraps." Or maybe I suddenly realized that my desire to follow my older sisters into the habit of going to school was one I had not thought through carefully enough. What it would mean, I quickly saw, was a loss of freedom and a commitment to a process I was unable then to fathom.

Still, eventually I came not just to admire Mrs. Dobbs but perhaps even to love her, despite her schoolmarmish ways, her odd phrases, her desire that we not be too spontaneous. After all, she cared for and about each one of us. She even seemed eager to hear our stories — winged on the fly sometimes — of our adventures out in the big world.

But from the moment I escaped from her classroom on that first morning, I knew that Mrs. Dobbs did not own me and that no person of authority would ever own me, however much allegiance I might pledge. My mother had the power and authority to take me back to school, but no longer was it possible for her or anyone else to control my mind or my heart fully. I wish every grown child on the planet could have walked out of school on the first day and been brought back by loving hands. Maybe none of those children, later in life, would have caved in to the temptation to make themselves giddy and brainless adherents of bad ideas or ecstatic followers of bad leaders. Maybe.

Mindfulness

THE DEAN STREET SCHOOL SIGN I READ EACH DAY COMING IN FROM RECESS.

When recess ended at Dean Street School, a loud bell summoned us to return from the boisterous (and girlsterous) playground to our classrooms.

Inevitably the ringing released this off-plumb but full-throated cry from kids running toward the doors: "Bell, bell, b-e-l. Bell, bell, b-e-l."

Yes, I know — and knew then — that it was a ridiculous misspelling (well, ridiculous unless you want to argue against the use of silent letters). But because it was ridiculous it alerted me to details. It caused me to pay attention. It made me notice things. It instilled in me — long before I had Buddhist friends who would name this attitude of curiosity for me — mindfulness.

So as I ran into what was clearly labeled "BOYS' ENTRANCE" above the three-paned windows that were themselves above the double doors, all framed by a Roman arch, I noticed, I paid attention. In that process I learned about the possessive case apostrophe after the "S". I'd like to think the habit of mindfulness has been deeply instilled into all Middle Americans, but I have to admit the evidence is at best uneven. Oh, many of us are accurate encyclopedias when it comes to sports trivia or celebrity marriages but our tolerance for sloppy and inarticulate communications and our willingness to let politicians tell us unchallenged lies convicts us.

Even all these decades later, however, I still cringe when I see apostrophes used incorrectly. I see people use them to make plurals — "The Smith's invite you to dinner." I see them in "it's" when the word meant is "its." I see them where they simply don't belong — "your's."

Every time it happens I wish the offender had attended Dean Street School and had regularly run into the GIRLS' or BOYS' entrance shouting "Bell, bell, b-e-l."

This attitude of mindfulness, of paying attention, of noticing has served me well as a journalist, but only when I remember to employ it. I learned it at the University of Missouri School of Journalism, but I got much better at it after the great Associated Press features writer Jules Loh came to Rochester, New York, in the late 1960s when I was a reporter there on the now-kaput afternoon newspaper, *The Times-Union*. Jules spent a day with some of us reporters instilling in us the idea of noticing details and using the relevant ones in our reporting. Pay attention, he said, and when you're done paying attention continue to pay attention.

Soon after that editors sent me to Auburn, New York, to do a story about a young man named Robert F. (Bobby) Stryker, who, in Vietnam, died when he threw himself on an exploding claymore mine, thus saving others in his unit.

My feature about Bobby Stryker was pressed down, shaken together, running over with details. Bell, bell, b-e-l.

And after the piece was printed I wondered this: Is there a BOYS' ENTRANCE to heaven? I hope not. I also hope to find the place full of other Middle Americans, some being mindful for maybe the first time.

Creativity

The day Billy Urch came home from kindergarten and brought all of his Halloween art with him I decided that I wanted to go to school and be creative. I happened to be at Billy's house that day because his mother was an occasional babysitter for us Tammeus kids. And seeing him come down the sidewalk wearing a witch's bonnet and carrying construction paper pumpkin art enthralled me.

It turned out that I had no artistic talent whatsoever. I couldn't draw squat, couldn't paint squat, couldn't even cut out things with scissors without ruining the project. But my attraction to being creative — one I shared with many Middle Americans — was in no way diminished just because the trees I drew looked like the Loch Ness Monster with fur.

Creativity, I soon learned, comes in many shapes, colors and styles. And Middle Americans have been among the most creative people in history. Either we created much of what we take for granted today — from high-def TV to iPads to e-books to breakthrough medicines to unique musical expressions to hybrid cars — or we accommodated the adoption of all such things and more into our lives in remarkably smooth ways.

My conception of the breadth of what constitutes creativity got widened one day in elementary school when my oldest sister, Karin, came home from junior high school and shared a funny twist on the old "Thirty Days Hath September" verse:

"Thirty Days Hath September,
April, June and no wonder.
All the rest eat peanut butter,
Except my grandma, and she drives a Buick."

Say what?

SINCE 1961

WOODSTOCK FINE ARTS ASSOCIATION

I WAS AMONG THOSE WHO HELPED TO REVIVE LIFE AT THE MORIBUND WOODSTOCK OPERA HOUSE, A MOVE THAT TURNED INTO THE WOODSTOCK FINE ARTS ASSOCIATION.

It was surrealistic nonsense, of course, but it was great fun. And I immediately began a lifelong love affair with wordplay. Indeed, I eventually made a living at it. For almost three decades I wrote a daily newspaper column in which wordplay had a leading role. I used puns. I made up words. I twisted words into new shapes. I especially loved coining portmanteau words — words that are a combination of two other words, like smog (I didn't make up that one), made up of smoke and fog. One of my favorite original portmanteau words is jackassembly, which I describe as almost being any legislative body, especially Congress.

But while I was creating word fun and, I hope, insight, other Middle Americans were creating all kinds of other things, approaches and ideas. They were coming up with new designs for almost everything, from automobiles to hairstyles, pens to homes, dresses to shoes. And although everyone knew there were boundaries — of taste, of decency, of moderation — we often crossed those boundaries in our explorations before finding something that was both new and acceptable. What did we reject? A small example. When I was writing the "Starbeams" column for *The Kansas City Star*, I often would think up quips and one-liners that, for reasons of taste, I couldn't use in a family newspaper. When, for instance, Billy Carter described himself as a "George Wallace Democrat" a few years after a gunman had injured Wallace so badly that he was confined to a wheelchair, I wrote a line that offered this definition of a George Wallace Democrat: "A Democrat without a leg to stand on." Of course it was too insensitive to use. And of course I didn't use it. But in the process of being creative you almost inevitably come up with things you have to discard. And yet you have to consider the killing of ideas as progress, not failure.

Even so, some of what we created was schlock that needed to be killed but wasn't: our toys, our television shows, our comic books, our poetry — oh, Lord, some of our poetry. But some of it has survived and morphed into things and ideas that continue to be socially useful. Even in various fields of scholarship we have contributed a lot through our creativity. We have, for instance, taken the beginnings of form criticism and other methods of biblical exegesis that were in their infancy and we have used them to achieve important insights about the writing that much of the world considers sacred and even divinely inspired. And we have taken early advances in science and helped move the world's understanding along. Science, in its pre-science form, was Aristotelian. Then that was replaced by a Newtonian approach, which later was overtaken (though not completely) by an Einsteinian approach until finally we are now in a post-Einsteinian world of String Theory, M Theory and other exotic ways of imagining how the creation is structured and how it works.

In classical and pop music we have stretched borders. We have created new expressions of literature and journalism. In travel we have helped the world move from rail and steam to jets and electric automobiles. And in communication we no longer must rely on the offsprings of the Pony Express but now can zing our words, our photos, our videos around the globe in nanoseconds.

All of this was because we learned early in life that creativity is both fun and appreciated, to say nothing of sometimes being profitable.

When I was in high school the old Opera House in Woodstock had been essentially unused for several years and was decaying. So some of us decided to see if we could get permission to get it reopened to offer plays to the community. With some adult help we laid the foundation for the 1961 creation of the Woodstock Fine Arts Association in the same building in which such folks as Paul Newman, Tom Bosley, Geraldine Page and Shelly Berman got their start in summer stock and winter stock plays. And we even produced at least one edition of what we called a fine arts magazine, *Cache*, which was full of the poetry and essays of teen-agers in Woodstock.

In all this we received adult encouragement. They channeled our creative impulses into productive activities. And that doesn't always happen.

I know, for instance, that there is something to the charge that our public schools often took — and still take — creative youngsters and beat the creativity out of them, forcing them to conform or fail. Indeed, that is truer than many people wish to acknowledge. I recall feeling in high school, in fact, that our teachers and administrators sometimes looked on creativity as an inconvenience, something that authorities found challenging. So our classes often seemed to be aimed at the level of C-minus students whose ability to think creatively had already been deadened or had never existed.

And yet when I look at how the world lived a hundred-plus years ago when my parents were born compared with how the world lives today I am astonished. Even late in their lives, my parents never had a cell phone, never banked by computer, never sent or received e-mail, never read an e-book, never heard of military drones killing Islamists in far-off lands.

As I say, some of our creativity has produced soul-crushing "reality" TV shows and pornography. Some has produced gambling games that have fleeced the poor. But on the whole I'm glad Mrs. Dobbs in kindergarten let Billy Urch — and, the next year me, once I got acclimated to staying in school — produce Halloween and Thanksgiving art. And I'm glad someone decided to announce that many of the months of the year eat peanut butter while my grandmother drives a Buick. It was just such silliness that set us free.

Fallout Shelters

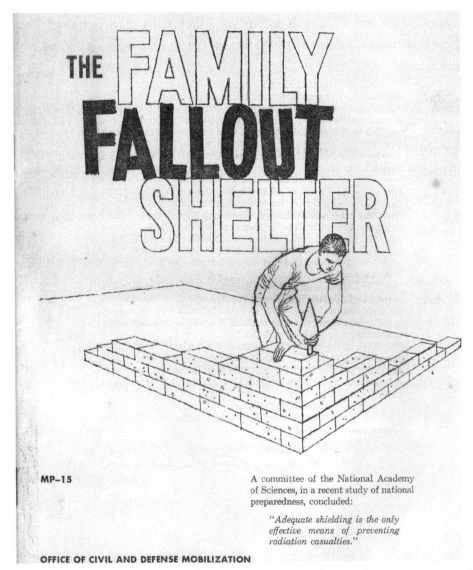

THE **FAMILY FALLOUT SHELTER**

MP-15

A committee of the National Academy of Sciences, in a recent study of national preparedness, concluded:

"Adequate shielding is the only effective means of preventing radiation casualties."

OFFICE OF CIVIL AND DEFENSE MOBILIZATION

THIS IS THE COVER OF THE PAMPHLET I FOUND IN MY PARENTS' HOME. IF THEY EVER READ IT, THEY ELECTED NOT TO BUILD A FALLOUT SHELTER.

The closest I ever came to owning a nuclear attack fallout shelter was my classroom desk at Dean Street School. In attack drills, we students would obediently get under those desks and kiss our little asses goodbye.

It's possible that some of us imagined that we could survive not just the initial explosion but also the radiation that would spread itself across the map like a prodigal plague without antidotes. But I doubt it. At least it seems to me now, many decades later, that many of us grade school kids found it at least a little hard to believe that *anyone* thought getting under a small desk to survive a nuclear attack was a sterling or effective idea.

What I do know is that this kind of magical thinking permeated almost every page of the 1950s Office of Civil Defense Mobilization (OCDM) booklet I still have, "The Family Fallout Shelter." For no reason better than morbid curiosity, I retrieved this publication from my parents' house after my mother died in 1996. Here's what Leo A. Hoegh, then OCDM director, wrote in the introduction to this thirty-two-page document, which was filled with architectural sketches and crazy hope: "The purpose of this booklet is to show how to escape death from fallout. Everyone, even those far from a likely target, would need shelter from fallout."

Everyone? Well, as a child, I would hear rumors about people building fallout shelters. Sometimes I'd see stories on the TV news showing someone actually constructing one. But I never knew anyone who built one, though in 1961 the government of McHenry County, of which Woodstock is the seat, authorized construction of a fallout shelter in the courthouse annex. My family certainly didn't follow suit and build one. Had we done so, knowing my father's cheapskate ways, I'm pretty sure it would have been cobbled together out of banged up, warped lumber found on the upper floor of the barn that served as our garage.

But Dad had other things to do, such as spraying carcinogenic insecticide on the apple and pear trees in our back-yard orchard. And, besides, we could always crawl under our desks at school. Still, the booklet is clear: "Fallout shelter is needed everywhere."

And the good news in the booklet? "Any mass of material between you and the fallout will cut down the amount of radiation that reaches you. Sufficient mass will make you safe." (And, no, that wasn't some slipped-in Catholic theology.)

The OCDM booklet is full of drawings showing people building shelters, and though inflation has knocked the May 1959 cost estimates into a cocked hat, the text says you can build a basement concrete block shelter for $150 to $200.

"This shelter would provide all the protection needed in most of the Nation," the pamphlet says. Nuclear war may disrupt your weekend, folks, but let's not panic.

However, by page 11, things start to look a little dicier — even, I'm sure, to adults reading this stuff back in the 1950s. There I see a drawing showing three people inside a basement fallout shelter, Father, Mother and Kid. Father is standing with one hand on his hip, facing the sitting Mother and Kid. Father looks stern, patriarchal. Clearly he is the king of the shelter and he's not happy about something. Perhaps he's ticked off that Kid, a boy of perhaps five years of age, is looking away from Father while Kid holds some kind of toy on which is written the word "log." Maybe Father is angry that Kid didn't give Father the log to be part of the construction material. But if things are going to start out this tense in the official model of a basement fallout shelter, God knows what might happen on Day 2 or Day 14 and on and on.

Later, on page 15, there's a drawing of an underground fallout shelter. Inside there's a bunk bed, and what appears to be a little girl, who is all tucked into the bottom bunk. But is this child going to get any sleep? No chance. Along with her in the room we find two men and a woman. One man — Is this Father? The milk man? — stands in the middle of the room and stares at the woman, who sits lounging on a sofa of some kind. The other man — Is this a captured Rooskie? — sits on a small stool staring at a wall. I'm thinking some enhanced interrogation techniques are being employed here. No wonder the girl isn't going to get any shuteye.

In almost every drawing, males stand (or build) while females sit or read. Is that how we middle-of-the-country, middle-of-the-century, Middle American boys learned the roles of males and females? Well, similar messages were everywhere then. Boys do. Girls watch what boys do — except when girls are with other girls, in which case they're allowed to jump rope or play jacks. It turns out that it takes a long time to unplug those old tapes, but many of us Middle Americans have at least tried.

By page 18 of this booklet, Leo and his OCDM people have started to move closer to reality in a section called "If An Attack Finds You Without A Prepared Shelter." But even here, the advice is not to kiss your ass goodbye. Nor is there any guidance to help you decide whether to shit or go blind. No, OCDM isn't giving up on survival easily. Why? Because "a family dwelling without a basement provides some natural shielding from fallout radiation. On the ground floor the radiation would be about half what it is outside."

Oh, and if you can get radio reception (you might need to extend an antenna outside the shelter, we're told) you can get official directions broadcast on 640 or 1240 AM, CONELRAD (Control of Electromagnetic Radiation). It was sort of the emergency broadcast system for the nuclear age.

Finally, figures 13 through 21 at the back of the booklet offer sketches and specific plans for building the fallout shelter of your nightmares.

Starting six months after my birth, with the successful test of an atomic bomb at the Trinity site in New Mexico in July 1945, we have lived with the possibility of being annihilated by nuclear weapons. And from shortly after the end of World War II until the Soviet Union collapsed in 1991, we were always aware that a big scary red enemy wanted to bury us, in Nikita Khrushchev's warm words.

So why weren't we more afraid back then? Indeed, I remember almost no fear about this at all. What gave us our swagger? Why did so many of us imagine that we'd never need to run to our fallout shelters or learn to speak Russian?

Maybe the answer is simple foolishness and naiveté by the metric ton. You can make a good case for that answer. But I prefer imagining that the bloated optimism running rampant then in Middle America, the idea that we could do anything we determined to do, the myths about the American Dream and our being a city set on a hill to give light to others — all that (some of which is, of course, hogwash) helped us be confident that we'd never have to figure out exactly what Leo and his OCDM folks meant in the Figure 15 directions for an above-ground, double-wall, six-person fallout shelter: "Paint or mop on a heavy coating of bituminous waterproofing after parapet walls have been completed." I still don't know what bituminous waterproofing or parapet walls are.

But by God I didn't die or catch a snoot full of radiation under my Dean Street School desk.

I will add only this: Kurt Vonnegut wrote a letter in 1961 to Harvey Kurtzman, founder of *MAD Magazine*, suggesting that there might well be a market for "shelter-hopping kits."[7] These kits would be sold to people "too lazy or too poor to build adequate fall-out shelters." Essentially, they were battering weapons, including explosives, "guaranteed to open any shelter yet recommended by Civil Defense."

Vonnegut, as usual, had correctly gauged the baffled spirit of the times. He added this in that letter: "Our town figured the appalling cost of building community shelters, decided instead to buy enough kits to take over the shelters of an adjoining town, thereby saving enough money to send the high school band to the next Orange Bowl game."

I wish I had lived in Vonnegut's town. The Woodstock Community High School Blue Streaks marching band in which I served in the color guard (oboe players don't march) once was sent fifty miles or so to Dyche Stadium (now Ryan Field) at Northwestern University in Evanston, Illinois, for "High School Band Day." As soon as the football field was filled with our band and a hundredyskillion other bands at halftime a colossal rainstorm hit, filling tubas and sending frightened flute players and drummers scrambling for shelter. Being at the edge of the field, I survived by quickly ducking under the bleachers with my fake rifle that I used to guard the colors. As far as I know, nothing of the sort ever happened to the band Vonnegut's town sent to the Orange Bowl.

Fame

MY SISTER MARY AND I MET INDIAN PRIME MINISTER JAWAHARLAL NEHRU IN NEW DELHI IN 1957.
THAT'S U.S. AMBASSADOR TO INDIA ELLSWORTH BUNKER LOOKING ON.

IN 1976, I LEFT THE DEMOCRATIC NATIONAL CONVENTION IN NEW YORK AFTER HELPING TO COVER JIMMY CARTER'S
NOMINATION AND FLEW TO WASHINGTON, D.C., TO INTERVIEW VICE PRESIDENT NELSON ROCKEFELLER IN ADVANCE OF
THE REPUBLICAN NATIONAL CONVENTION LATER THAT SUMMER IN KANSAS CITY. — PHOTO USED WITH THE PERMISSION
OF THE WHITE HOUSE COUNSEL'S OFFICE AND THE NATIONAL ARCHIVES AND RECORDS ADMINISTRATION.

"My first week in Rome passed in a daze. I could not yet believe I had left behind me, like a room abruptly locked in my absence, the bucolic town of Woodstock, Illinois — the town my father once likened to 'a wax flower under a bell of glass in the paisley and gingham county of McHenry.'" — In My Father's Shadow: A Daughter Remembers Orson Welles, by Chris Welles Feder; Algonquin Books of Chapel Hill, 2009; Page 75

Sometimes the number of famous people I've met, interviewed or at least seen in person seems remarkable to me: George H.W. Bush, Jimmy Carter, Bill Clinton, Richard Nixon, Gerald Ford, Lady Bird Johnson, Rosalyn Carter, Nancy Reagan, Walter Mondale, Al Gore, John Glenn, Neil Armstrong, Bob Dole, Nelson Rockefeller, Robert F. Kennedy, Martin Luther King Sr., Jesse Jackson, Paul Newman, Jawaharlal Nehru, Indira Gandhi, Mick Jagger, Elvis Presley, Mahalia Jackson, the Rev. Sun Myung Moon, Pearl Bailey, Warren Buffett, Billy Graham, Eddie Fisher, governors, senators, congressmen galore, more sports figures than I can count, from George Brett to Ernie Banks (my childhood hero) to Muhammad Ali, Willie Mays, Yogi Berra, Len Dawson, Buck O'Neill, Cal Ripkin, Dick Butkus and more.

And in no case was I intimidated or star-struck. Woodstock, Illinois, may seem like an oddly out-of-the-way place to encounter celebrities, but it turns out that we ran into more than our share there, though my list in the previous paragraph is due in large measure to my career in journalism. And I suspect many Middle Americans also have run across lots of famous people. For instance, my sister Barbara once met a famous patient on the same floor where she was recovering from surgery at Mayo Clinic in Rochester, Minnesota: William Lawrence Boyd, who played Hopalong Cassidy on television.

The famous names attached to Woodstock lore include actor Orson Welles, who attended Todd School there; Chester Gould, the creator of the Dick Tracy comic strip, who lived there; Eugene Debs, who was jailed in Woodstock in the 1890s as a result of the Pullman strike and who became a famous member of the Socialist Party; plus all the getting-their-start actors and actresses who spent time in summer and winter stock performing at the old Opera House. This list included Paul Newman — who, with his first wife Jackie, lived with my family in our West South Street house for part of a year — Geraldine Page, Tom Bosley, Shelley Berman and more. Indeed, when Bill Murray and Andie MacDowell came to Woodstock to film the classic 1993 movie "Groundhog Day," people from Woodstock became friends with them, further demystifying the cult of celebrity. They didn't just stand around and ogle the cast, they brought blankets and heaters from their houses to keep the cast members warm when they were shooting the film outdoors in cold weather. They acted like useful, hospitable Middle Americans, in other words.

Beyond all of those people there were Woodstock's own famed honorable mentions. One was Guy Curtright, who played outfield for the Chicago White Sox from 1943 to 1946, before becoming a coach at Woodstock Community High School. In 1945, Guy tied for the Sox team lead in homers for the season with…wait for it, four (count it, four). His four homers tied the number smacked that year by the mortal Johnny Dickshot. You could look it up. No, really. You could look up Johnny Dickshot. (I added that last sentence just to write Dickshot again. That sentence, too.)

John Strohm was another honorable mention in the Woodstock fame department. John was editor of the *Ford Almanac* and a journalist who managed to get behind the Iron Curtain and into both Russia and China soon after World War II to write such books as *Just Tell the Truth: The Uncensored Story of the Russian People Today.* John and his wife Lillian (who, after John's death, dated — or at least hung out with — Orville Redenbacher, the popcorn king) were among my parents' best friends. I remember watching the 1952 Republican National Convention on a TV at the Strohm house, partly because, as I recall, John helped write some of Dwight D. Eisenhower's speeches on farm policy. By the way, one of John and Lillian Strohm's sons, David, now tells fabulous stories about Woodstock and, more broadly, Middle Americans, on his "Boomkids" website.[8]

In the end, Middle Americans are more impressed with people's accomplishments and attitudes toward life than they are with their fame. In fact, among us Middle Americans there is something of a disdain for people who are famous merely for being famous — the Paris Hiltons of the planet, the Kardashians.

Some of what I'm saying about this is personal and not representative of all Middle Americans, but my disinterest in celebrity is one reason I (unlike one of my sisters) pay no attention to such outlets as *People Magazine* and other shrines to immodesty. Oh, yes, there are some Middle Americans who watch every broadcast of "American Idol," who wait for the latest celebrity news on "TMZ" or "Entertainment Tonight." But mostly the cultural trash that such outlets offer bypasses my radar screen and the radar screens of many Middle Americans. Many of us — though not enough to kill all this junk — frankly don't give a damn.

But show us the sacrificial accomplishments of some of the people featured on CNN's "Heroes" presentations or on NBC Nightly News' "Making a Difference" segment and we're there applauding. And not just applauding but also wondering whether we might be called to do something similar. We tend to hear a lot of "shoulds" as we go through the day, and at least some of them are worth paying attention to.

We'll be gracious to the rich and famous when we run across them but we'll be mostly unimpressed unless they've used their wealth and position to help repair the wounded world — a phrase my Jewish friends know as *tikkun olam.* A great example was the late great Middle American Adele Hall (1931-2013), daughter-in-law of Joyce Hall, the founder of Hallmark Cards. She was unpretentious and an extraordinarily giving person. And it was more than *noblesse oblige.* When she died no one — literally no one — in private or public had an unkind word to say about her, as her pastor affirmed to me in a private conversation.

So give us the Adele Halls and we're interested — enough to try to emulate them. Give us the Paris Hiltons and we'd rather read newspaper pages full of legal notices about property foreclosures. I wouldn't call this snobbish, though others might. I would call it having our heads screwed on right, our values and priorities in order.

AFTER THE HEBRON GREEN GIANTS BOYS HIGH SCHOOL BASKETBALL TEAM WON THE ILLINOIS STATE CHAMPIONSHIP IN 1952, THEY PARADED THROUGH THE SQUARE IN WOODSTOCK AND I WATCHED. — PHOTO COURTESY OF MCHENRY COUNTY HISTORICAL SOCIETY.

Among the most worthwhile famous people I ever saw in Woodstock were the members of the 1952 Hebron, Illinois, Green Giants basketball team — a small handful of guys from a school containing about 100 students. In a time when there were no divisions into various classes by size of school, the Green Giants won the Illinois state high school basketball championship. They paraded through Woodstock on their way home. I was seven years old. I sat on the fire escape steps of the Opera House and applauded, knowing even at that age that I was seeing fame that resulted from terrific effort and accomplishment.

Put on a parade today in Woodstock or anywhere else, one featuring Paris Hilton, Britney Spears, Ryan Seacrest, Lindsay Lohan, Snooki, Paula Abdul, Carmen Electra, Dr. Phil and all the Kardashian sisters, and I wouldn't see it except by complete inadvertence. And neither would most Middle Americans. Well, unless, just for fun, we wanted to brag that one day we were in the presence of the most pointless celebrities ever assembled in one spot.

The Church Basement

WHEN I WAS A BOY THIS WAS FIRST PRESBYTERIAN CHURCH. THAT CONGREGATION HAS BUILT A NEW BUILDING AT THE NORTH EDGE OF WOODSTOCK AND THIS ONE NOW IS OWNED BY ANOTHER CHURCH.

Just inside the front doors of the (now former) First Presbyterian Church in Woodstock was a small vestibule where people would take off their coats and prepare to enter the sanctuary through a nearby door. But there was also another door there. It led to the basement.

That's where some of my young friends and I, including the preacher's son, kept cigarettes and girlie magazines in a hidden space behind the furnace. What fine boys we were.

I no longer remember which one of us discovered this secret gathering spot or exactly when. And my recollection is that only four or five of us ever knew about it. This would have been while we were in junior high, probably, when we were beginning to imagine what it might be like to commit adult sins.

I had essentially zero interest in the cigarettes. I didn't take up smoking until my senior year in high school. I smoked through college and a bit afterward but gave it up one evening when I couldn't think of a single reason to commit suicide in slow motion. I was driving my car near the University of Rochester in upstate New York that evening and, in an act of heroic commitment and misdemeanor littering, I reached into my shirt pocket, grabbed a half-empty pack of cigarettes and tossed it into a ditch along the side of the road. I'm sorry. If it's still there I'll come pick it up and dispose of it properly. But the memory makes me wonder how other Middle Americans quit smoking, as many of them did.

I never made a similar commitment to abandon females. I was hooked on them from kindergarten on, though I recall being well aware even as a fourteen-year-old that the women who were appearing naked in magazines were some kind of fantasy meant to make men also look at the accompanying ads for cars and clothes and whatnot. Clearly those pictures exploited women, but hardly any of the fourteen-year-olds I knew then imagined in his wildest dreams that such beautifully air-brushed women would be interested in us.

So the question is this: What was really happening down in the basement of that church building when a handful of boys moving through puberty gathered to look at pictures, talk and smoke? I know the answer now, though I didn't then. The answer is: Church was happening.

Church, at its core, is about relationship — vertically with the divine and horizontally with other humans. We boys were figuring out the horizontal part of that in a building where people practiced the vertical part together. Together. That's the key. We were comrades, plotters, secret-keepers. We were learning to trust one another, to rely on one another, to have one another's back. That later turned out to be a foundational Middle American value. And it would be important for those times in our teen years when our parents misunderstood us profoundly and we needed a sympathetic ear or when our school basketball or football team failed miserably, sometimes due to the incompetence of those of us in the church basement gang.

So, in the end, we learned about the importance of community by sneaking around. It's a crazy way to discover life's important lessons, but there was a fair amount about life in the middle of the century in the middle of the country that now, in retrospect, seems a little crazy.

Who, for instance, decided that teen-agers being able to drive big cars around and around and around The Square was a measure of coolness? Crazy.

I'm not sorry even today that I hid in a church basement with buddies and read girlie magazines. But I am sorry we felt that for some purposes we needed a clandestine community instead of having available an above-ground community that would allow us to explore answers to our difficult questions and to grow up finding good answers to them. Oh, we had a little of that in youth groups, sports teams, scouts and so on. But nobody in those groups ever told us why it was perfectly natural for teen-age boys to be so interested in looking at pictures of naked women. We had to figure out all of that for ourselves, from each other. So no doubt part of what we figured out was wrong and stupid and hurtful.

Still, I'm glad we found that corner of the church basement we could call our own. And I'm glad we never had to explain what we were doing down there to any girls. We had enough to feel ashamed about without that.

Faith

Woodstock in the 1950s was a landslide for Protestantism. Oh, there was a substantial Catholic population, a handful of Christian Science adherents, some Unitarians comingled in a Congregationalist church and one Jewish family, the members of which went to Chicago when they wanted to attend Shabbat services. But mostly the Methodists, Presbyterians, Lutherans and a few others were dominant.

As was the case in much of Middle America, churches in Woodstock were the center of a lot of social and civic life. Some Cub and Boy Scout troops gathered in them along with some civic clubs, such as the Kiwanis or Rotary. Their own internal life included regular potluck dinners, picnics, youth groups, men's clubs, women's circles, travelogues and

THIS WAS MY CONFIRMATION CLASS IN APRIL 1958 AT FIRST PRESBYTERIAN CHURCH IN WOODSTOCK.

other excuses (even beyond weddings and funerals) to gather in community and actually be community. Not everyone was in church on Sunday morning, but those who weren't became outsiders. Sixty-plus years later it's all different. Instead of almost no stores being open on Sundays back then, now almost everything is open, and youth sports venues are full of kids and their cheering parents and grandparents on Sunday mornings.

In fact, the whole religious landscape of the United States is different today. No doubt Woodstock still is predominantly Protestant, but Protestants no longer make up a majority of Americans, having slipped just below the fifty percent level in the latest surveys. Christians still make up a three-fourths majority of Americans, but ever since President Lyndon B. Johnson signed immigration reform into law in 1965, millions of Hindus, Muslims, Sikhs, Jains, Buddhists and Zoroastrians as well as Christians from different traditions than those found in the states have come to America's shores. More than that, the number of religiously unaffiliated people has grown to the point that they now make up about 20 percent of the population.

We Middle Americans have adapted to all of this, but some not nearly as well as others. While some of us have been active in interfaith groups that promote religious harmony and understanding, others have bought into fear and have promoted prejudices that have acquired such labels as Islamophobia

37

and antisemitism. And almost across the board there has been biblical and theological illiteracy that is astonishing in its breadth and depth. This self-inflicted wound caused Boston University scholar Stephen Prothero to write this in his 2007 book, *Religious Literacy: What Every American Needs to Know – And Doesn't:* "…the average voter knows embarrassingly little about Christianity and other religions."[9] It's not quite that most Americans think Joan of Arc was Noah's wife, but it's almost that bad.

Worse, ignorance of our own religious traditions and those of others means that our ability to help the world live in religious harmony is severely compromised. As writer and social critic Os Guinness notes in *The Global Public Square*, ". . .the combination of the Western lack of faith and the Western lack of understanding of faiths renders the West clumsily incompetent when face to face with the raging faiths on steroids in other parts of the world."[10]

I'm certainly more sensitive to all of this than most Middle Americans because I've spent part of my journalism career covering religion. I still do a daily blog called "Faith Matters" on *The Kansas City Star*'s website and I write columns for *The Presbyterian Outlook* and *The National Catholic Reporter*. So as far as Middle Americans and religious literacy goes, I'm an outlier. I get that. But that doesn't make our widespread ignorance about matters of religion any less disappointing, especially when you remember that polls consistently show that more than 90 percent of Americans say they believe in God (though as pollster George Barna notes, our ideas about God are so varied that, in effect, Americans believe in about 300 million different gods).

No doubt I was being unfair, in an arrogant teen-age sort of way, when I concluded in high school that all churches were full of hypocrites and that I couldn't wait to abandon that ship of fools. A dozen years after I walked away from the church when I left high school I came to acknowledge that I was one of those hypocrites and I needed help. So I found my way back to church, back to faith, back to healthy doubt.

But surely my judgment about hypocrisy in the church was based on something real, and I now think of people who then were engaged in destructive gossip, who were unfaithful in their marriages, who sought to take unfair advantage of people in business situations and on and on. Yes, there also were wonderful people serving as volunteers in great causes, giving and doing what they could to repair the world, encouraging and comforting others. Among those people were my parents. People joked about them that they made a living on dollar-a-year jobs. But teen-age antennae are sharply tuned to hypocrisy and I found plenty of it in Woodstock.

On the whole, however, people in Woodstock from different Christian traditions then seemed to get along without major conflict. The only scarring example of the opposite I recall was when our Presbyterian pastor told us in 1960 that if John F. Kennedy were elected our first Catholic president the pope would run the country. Even back then I suspected that this was nonsense, but it came from a man of authority and no doubt his prejudice poisoned plenty of minds — at least until JFK was in office and the prediction proved unfounded.

In the end, Middle Americans who grew up in the middle of the last century wound up with a faith that was both simple, in the good sense of that word, and simplistic. They prayed for parking spaces for themselves and believed God could spare them from natural disasters if God wanted to. They were properly baffled by the many mysteries of faith but willing to use clichés (some of them quite unbiblical) to explain (apparently to their satisfaction) what otherwise made little sense: God helps those who helps themselves; your dead loved one is in a better place now; God needed a sweet angel in heaven so he took your child; let go and let God; our thoughts and prayers are with you; the Lord giveth and the Lord taketh away…

Middle Americans have become the core of the reality that America is one of the most religious countries in the world, even if we have trouble explaining what we believe and why because of a tendency at times to live unexamined lives. Among Middle Americans are people who understand that all language is metaphorical and that religious language is especially so, who know that you can take the Bible seriously or you can take it literally but you can't do both.

But there also are Middle Americans who believe the Bible is in all ways inerrant, that somehow Earth is only a few thousand years old, that God created the world in six literal days, that evolution is a hoax and on and on. Some of these gullible people became targets for such theological nincompoops as Pat Robertson and his "700 Club" on TV. As Duke Divinity School scholar Kate Bowler reported in her 2013 book, *Blessed: A History of the American Prosperity Gospel*, that show "earned strong ratings from educated, middle-class, and Midwestern viewers, making him the prophet of middle America."[11] Oh, my. Say it ain't so.

And in between are the people whom Princeton Theological Seminary religion scholar Kenda Creasy Dean calls therapeutic moralistic deists,[12] who essentially think a relatively disinterested God just wants everyone to play nicely with others. Middle Americans all.

I'm glad Middle Americans form the foundation of religious life in America, but I wish they knew better what they were talking about and had as much interest in soteriology and eschatology as they do in "American Idol," the current NFL standings and whether Justin Beiber is a virgin. Lord, forgive us.

Socialized Medicine

I WAS ALMOST 11 YEARS OLD AT THE TIME OF THIS SCHOOL FORM DOCUMENTING MY HEALTH.

As I write this, I am looking at documentary evidence that when I was seven years and one month old and in first grade in February 1952, I was forty-nine and seven-eighths inches tall and weighed fifty-five and a half pounds. This now nearly useless information is found on a mimeographed sheet filled out at Dean Street School by the school nurse.

That sheet does not reveal who the school nurse was, though on a different sheet, filled out on December 16, 1955, when I was in fifth grade, the nurse was listed as G.G. Sailer. (The first G stood for Gertrude.) By this time I had begun to sprout. I was fifty-eight and a half inches tall and weighed eighty-one pounds, though I'm guessing that total counted the heavy flannel shirt and the weighty blue jeans with felt (or something) lining that we cool boys wore in the bitter northern Illinois winters. So probably I was barely seventh-five pounds.

I had pneumonia three times before fifth grade, so it's possible to imagine that the medical examination I was given in 1952 showing X's by "Throat" and "Glands" may have pointed to something like a precursor to the disease that would cause me to miss a chunk of second grade, when my teacher, Cora White, would stop by the house and tutor me. By contrast, my 1955 exam conducted by G.G. Sailer says I had a "negative examination," and deserved X's by nothing. I was, apparently, a stunning specimen of American boyhood. I was fast, too. I could outrun almost any kid in school, and sometimes needed to.

What these two sheets — plus a one-page record my mother kept ("Immunization Record — Billy Tammeus") — represent is evidence of the long history of our government's involvement in the health of its citizens. For what else is an examination by a paid public school nurse if not what some people contemptuously dismiss as socialized medicine?

On the basis of the wording on these sheets, I would argue that not only was it socialized medicine, it was also paternalistic interference with a family's God-given right to send sickly and contagious children to school.

The note to parents on both sheets, separated by five years, is exactly the same, except that in the 1955 version, someone has added a "please." Here's what they say:

<u>PARENTS</u>: Please inspect your children every morning before sending them to school.

1. Do they show symptoms of contagious disease such as: inflamed eyes, coughing, swelling about neck, sore throat, unusual paleness, fever, rash, nausea, and vomiting? If so, keep them home in bed.
2. Are they rested?
3. Have they eaten a good breakfast?
4. Are they clean and neat?
5. Have they brushed their teeth?

ALL CHILDREN SHOULD BE IMMUNIZED AGAINST SMALLPOX, DIPTHTHERIA, WHOOPING COUGH, AND TETANUS.

Now, it's true that most of my immunizations were done by a private physician, though I do remember getting polio vaccine in school — on a sugar cube. But clearly the state, through the school district, not only had an interest in my physical well-being but had specific tasks that my parents were ordered to follow in helping to meet the state's goals: "keep them home in bed."

Woodstock and McHenry County, of which it is the seat, traditionally have been landslides for Republicanism — though not the strait-jacket, uncompromising Republicanism of the modern and much-regretted Tea Party era but, rather, the Republicanism represented by such thoughtful and decent human beings as Dwight D. Eisenhower. This kind of reasonable Republicanism was happy to make room for government involvement in the health care of our children and even in the government giving not just advice but orders to parents about how to help with this task. Nobody took Gertrude Sailer to court to tell her to quit butting in.

We did not call it a private-public coalition, but that's what it was. In many ways it became a model for how Middle Americans like me came to think about government. We chose our government. Our government was us and is us. We knew who the agents of government were and could talk with them directly if need be. Mom could ask the school nurse what she saw about my throat and glands that needed attention. Dad could call up A. B. McConnell, our state representative, or Bob McClory, our congressional representative, and talk about whatever needed to be talked about. I doubt that Dad or Mom ever contributed more than $5 to either politician. More likely $0.

So when Middle Americans like me look at government today it's painful to think that so many of its agents are beholden not to the voters but to the groups that contribute the huge amounts of money that must be raised to win a campaign. If Gertrude Sailer were to do an examination on the body politic today, my guess is that she'd put X's by a long list of matters that "Need Attention."

(By the way, speaking of medical matters, I also am in possession of evidence that my 1945 circumcision, performed at what then was called the Woodstock Public Hospital, cost $2.50. Plus tips? Don't ask.)

Illness, Death

THIS IS THE FRONT DOOR TODAY OF THE HOSPITAL IN WOODSTOCK WHERE I WAS BORN IN 1945.

Three times as a child I contracted pneumonia. One time the case was serious enough, I'm told, that there was a least a little fear that I might not survive. Hello, Mr. Death.

But our physician would come to our house, sit on the edge of my temporary bed in the downstairs room we called the office and do his magic. Somehow it always worked and I survived. And when I was at least well enough to sit up and pay attention, sometimes whoever was my teacher would come by and tutor me so I wouldn't be far behind when I finally returned to the classroom. My second grade teacher, Cora White, who lived just a few houses up West South Street toward the high school from us, spent a fair amount of time at our house doing just that, bless her old-maid heart.

About the time all that was going on polio was striking our generation. When we'd visit my maternal grandparents — Swedish immigrants who lived a hundred miles south of us — they would say to us with their never-lost accent, "Now ven you go outside, vear a yacket so you don't get polio."

Who knew polio was so easy to ward off? Just a jacket — well, yacket — apparently would do.

Whispers of our mortality were all around us. Some examples: A child named Karen who lived on my street died from what I recall was some kind of meningitis. One of the Zimmerman boys was killed by a bullet accidently fired by one of his brothers. When I was in junior high school, Cathy Still's brother Dee succumbed to an illness I no longer can name. Several of the high school kids who drove twenty minutes to Wisconsin, where the legal beer-drinking age was eighteen, died in car wrecks on the way home. Leukemia got our classmate Tom Neville when we were sophomores in high school (see my chapter on courage). When I was in eighth grade our pastor led a funeral in our church for Johnny Stompanato, the bad-boy playboy brother of one of our church members. Johnny had died at the hands of actress Lana Turner's daughter. And when I was five years old or so, my mother plucked me from our front yard, where I was playing, and made me walk across the street with her to attend the in-home wake of a woman we called Grandma Moore — the first dead body I'd ever seen. I tried to get out of it by telling Mom I didn't want to go because I didn't want or need to see an old dead lady naked. (Why do dead people need clothes, after all? Good reasoning for a kid.) But Mom explained the tradition of dressing the dead to protect their dignity. And I went.

I HELPED MY MOTHER PICK OUT THIS HEADSTONE, NOW LOCATED IN OAKLAND CEMETERY IN WOODSTOCK.

Many of us Middle Americans, thus, grew up knowing we were not immortal. This differs a bit from the currently widespread American idea that death is optional. Death was a relatively constant companion for Middle Americans as kids. The dead in my life included my paternal grandmother, who perished of abdominal cancer when I was eight years old. My paternal grandfather, who was quite a bit older than Grandma Tammeus, lasted until age 83, dying when I was a freshman in high school. All of this says nothing about the pets we watched die, including our deeply loved Siberian husky Sitka, who finally had to be put down. All six members of my family sat around the kitchen table that day and cried — even my father, who generally kept up the silly masculine pretension that men shouldn't (and, thus, don't) cry.

What seems now mostly inexplicable is that we Middle Americans, marinated from childhood in the culture of death, seem to have helped turn Americans into ardent death deniers. First we quit having wakes in our homes. No doubt the funeral industry was to some extent behind that change simply for reasons of convenience — for funeral directors — and profit. But we let it happen. Instead, most of the visitations after death began to take place in sterile funeral homes, which had no connection to the life of the person in the casket (or urn). Even a growing number of the funerals themselves — which became disembodied memorial services[13] — moved out of churches or other houses of worship to funeral homes.

Each time we took one of these steps, we backed away from the reality of death — even while we watched untold numbers of people die on TV and in the movies. And as we moved away from death we began to imagine that — or at least act as if — death happens not to us but only to people we don't know.

When we'd attend memorial services we'd find, at most, a beautiful urn up front containing the cremains of whoever died. Or sometimes just a picture of the deceased. And even when we went to graveside services to bury a body in a casket, the ground was all covered with fake green turf and often the casket was not lowered into the earth and covered again until after everyone had left. (What I'm describing was predominantly a Christian, especially Protestant — not a Jewish — phenomenon. The Jews mostly still respect death and understand the need to live with it.)

For Middle Americans, however, the necessary rituals of death eventually became pretty, clean, remote and decorated with fragrant flowers.

This nonsense went radically against the grain of the upbringing that many of us experienced. But perhaps what happened is not so surprising. After all, few of us raise our own food any more. Our children and grandchildren grow up thinking sweet corn comes from Price Chopper, Safeway or Kroger. And we mostly don't repair our own cars anymore, either, given that they've become computerized mysteries to us. We don't cut our own hair or that of members of our family. We hire people to clean our houses. We get a neighborhood kid to shovel snow off our driveway and mow our yard.

So increasingly we subcontract out life, outsourcing it to others for pay. Our avoidance of even talk about death falls into this pattern. It's one of the terrible legacies we are leaving the country. We Middle Americans owe the country an apology for this one.

Come to my funeral. I plan to have my body present and to have people talk about the reality of death and God's promise of resurrection. Then I've asked to be cremated and my ashes buried in the lawn of my church, Second Presbyterian of Kansas City, Missouri. And people who attended my funeral — a funeral, not a memorial service — will be invited back to watch my ashes mix with the earth. It's a funeral you will remember. Heck, I may even remember it. You will pay respects to the power and finality of death — as well as to the Christian doctrine of the resurrection of the body, which is quite a different idea from the old Greek notion of the immortal soul. Nothing about me — or anyone — is immortal. If God wants to be in an eternal relationship with me, that'll be up to God, who alone is immortal.

When people leave my funeral I hope they will think of e.e. cummings' poem with no title beyond its first line, "Buffalo Bill's defunct," and especially the last line, "how do you like your blueeyed boy/Mister Death". Cummings didn't end that poem with a question mark, but I'll end the next sentence with one because death is full of mysteries. Is our fear of mystery why we've degenerated into avoiding it? And what kind of legacy is that to leave? We Middle Americans haven't done well with this matter and I'm sorry about that. In fact, it makes me ill.

Change

WHEN I WAS A BOY, THIS WAS THE MCHENRY COUNTY COURTHOUSE ON THE SQUARE IN WOODSTOCK. AFTER I LEFT TOWN A NEW COURTHOUSE WAS BUILT AT THE EDGE OF TOWN. NOW THIS IS AN UNDERUSED LANDMARK THAT NO ONE QUITE KNOWS WHAT TO DO WITH.

"Life certainly is full of uncertainties. We all have to learn how to bend." — In a March 14, 1989, letter to my family from my mother, who the next day bent into her seventy-seventh year.

Crawling toward consciousness in my temporary downstairs bed, which was pushed against a wall of the room we called the office in our 415 West South Street house, I saw something so astonishing out the window that I was sure I had slept for a month, maybe more.

It was snowing.

When I first got sick with my second or third case of childhood pneumonia, the weather outside had been lovely. A warm fall. Green leaves not yet turned. But now this. What was happening? How had I lost my sense of time, my sense of context?

I stared out the window for several minutes, and some gear in my brain shifted. Life, I knew now, was now unpredictable, unreliable, capable of shocking surprises. It would be good to know this because it turned out that from then on, that's pretty much how life behaved for me and for most Middle Americans.

I don't know how other Middle Americans learned to factor in what Alvin Toffler labeled "future shock" in his 1970 book of that title[14], but I got alerted in my elementary school bout of pneumonia that there were surprises out there. My weather-change stunner, of course, had nothing to do with the kinds of scientific, medical, sociological, economic, political and other changes that would characterize our era. But it did help prepare me for the idea of sudden, unexpected, category-altering change.

And without such preparation no Middle American could make sense of what the world would throw at us — or, in some cases, what we would throw at the world.

I like to be warned that change is coming, that life is about to shift in this way or that. But I know that sometimes change happens like an astonishing, dumbfounding, flabbergasting explosion in the soft belly of the night. That's what happened when the 9/11 hijackers murdered my nephew, Karleton D.B. Fyfe, along with nearly three thousand other people in September 2001. It's what happened when JFK was assassinated in 1963, when RFK and MLK were in 1968.

But the difference was that even though those were cataclysmic, horrifying events that wounded our souls, they were not outside the realm of what we knew was possible. We knew, at least in a general way, to expect surprises, even if we had no hint about their content, architecture or timing. In some ways we already had imagined five-hundred-point down days on the Dow Jones Industrial Average, already taken into account the possibility of a man landing on the moon, of Princess Diana dying in a car wreck in Paris, of finding the smoking gun on the White House tapes that would cause Richard Nixon to quit, of Bobby Thomson's "shot heard 'round the world" home run in 1951 to win the National League pennant. We didn't know those possibilities in detail, of course, but at least we had a general sense that such things could happen. Shock happens. Awe happens. No surprise there except the particulars of the surprise itself.

As each shock came along, we became more shock-proof, less likely to go off screaming incoherently, more able to face the incredibly relentless and high-speed express train of change that almost daily sought to run us over. The strange thing, perhaps, is that being nearly shock-proof did not deaden our souls. Rather, it made us ready to be ready to be ready. In other words, it quickened us, not unlike the way a shortstop goes into his half-crouch just before the pitcher flings the ball toward home plate.

Harry Truman beats Tom Dewey in 1948? TV quiz shows turn out to be fixed? North Korea invades South Korea? The Russians have the H-bomb? Rock Hudson is gay? There's yet another government shutdown?

We handled all that and more, all the breaking news of scandal and war, scientific breakthroughs and natural disasters, all the serial killers and children dying in school fires, all the flashpoints, bulletins, tornado warnings, the product recalls and the sudden cries of "TIM-BER!" from one aghast voice after another.

We Middle Americans figured out early in our lives that we needed to widen our stance, put our faces toward the gale and hang on. As often as not, we ourselves were contributing to the nor'easters of change, the shocks, the double-take developments of our era. It was our own people who were moving us from vinyl records to eight-track tape to cassette tape to compact disks to MP3 players to Pandora music from the cloud. It was Middle Americans who were replacing crank phones with candlestick phones and then wall-mounted or standard desk phones that connected directly to the "number please" operators and then rotary dial phones and then Trimline punch-button phones and cordless home phones and phones with answering machines and mobile phones and MagicJack apps on our iPads that let us call home from Israel or Canada for free.

We who were ready for any surprise also tried to cut down on surprise by inventing caller I.D. for our phones so we wouldn't waste our time talking to this or that solicitor, this or that thief of our precious minutes, our hours, our energy, our patience.

In the end, of course, we sometimes still were surprised by surprise. Who could predict the fall of the Berlin Wall, the explosion of the Challenger space shuttle, the blue dress Monica Lewinsky saved because it carried a stain from Bill Clinton's sperm, the election of a black president before a female president? Who?

But the possibility of astonishment itself did not and does not astonish us. So we are steady, calm, unfazed by the reality that disasters happen, even though those disasters can and do make our hearts go soft and make us want to help. Our resolve in the face of the inevitability of shock has given us a confidence that we can overcome almost anything, including three cases of childhood pneumonia, even if sometimes we can't.

The Farm

CORN FIELDS LIKE THIS ONE IN ILLINOIS ARE PART OF THE DNA OF MIDDLE AMERICANS.

My parents grew up on Illinois farms about a hundred miles apart. My maternal grandparents, Swedish immigrants, farmed at the edge of Streator, Illinois, until they were too old to manage it anymore, but they lived on their farm until they died, each at or near age ninety. My paternal grandparents farmed just outside Delavan, Illinois, between Peoria and Springfield, until they finally moved into town and turned the farm over to their youngest son, my Dad's brother Lawrence. Grandpa Tammeus, whose German-immigrant parents had farmed that land before him, was well into his seventies then. Grandma died of cancer in her sixties only a year or two after the move.

Although my nuclear family did not live on a farm, my father for many years was a farm adviser, or county extension agent, attached to the University of Illinois. And our garage in Woodstock, just a few blocks from The Square, was an old barn, in which I raised chickens and near which I regularly helped raise a garden and other crops, sometimes as part of a 4-H club project.

Like many Middle Americans, my DNA has farming all through it. Mine may run a bit deeper than some, but it doesn't take long to connect most Middle Americans to some kind of farm experience or background. What difference has that made to us? And what difference has it made to the country?

For one thing, it has meant that we Middle Americans have been dependable, mostly. I am thinking of the model of my Uncle Lawrence, who had dairy cattle for years on the Delavan farm where my father grew up. Lawrence had to be there twice a day to milk them. He simply couldn't miss a milking — and didn't. As for me, I followed Lawrence's example in this way: In more than thirty-six years of full-time employment at *The Kansas City Star*, I missed only three and a half days due to illness. And I never missed turning in a daily column in the twenty-seven years that I wrote one.

My work history is not unusual among Middle Americans. Oh, for sure there have been some slackers in our midst, irresponsible people who'd call in sick so they could go to the beach or sleep all day. But mostly those were the exceptions. Mostly we were afflicted by almost-terminal cases of the Protestant Work Ethic. Mostly we got our perfect attendance pins or retirement gold watches (well, neither of the two watches and one clock I got as a long-time *Kansas City Star* employee is gold, but they're still pretty good time keepers).

And this longevity in our work places meant that eventually we knew where the bodies were buried. We served as the institutional memories of the organizations that employed us or the ones we simply joined out of personal interest — the Lions or Kiwanis clubs, the Bible study groups, the book or garden clubs, the bowling leagues. We guided the newcomers so they'd understand the culture into which they had dropped. We went as far up the organizational ladder as our skills and drive would take us and we didn't move from job to job or career to career nearly as much as our children have — though we often sympathized with those later moves when we discovered to our chagrin that loyalty to the company eventually came not to be reciprocated by company loyalty to us. But by the time that new ethic of non-loyalty was widespread, we weren't much interested in picking up and starting over somewhere else anyway.

How did the farms in our personal history teach us all this? Partly through the stories we watched unfold, partly through the stories we told.

One day Grandpa Helander drove his big red Farmall tractor from the field to the shed where he kept it overnight. He pulled in a little too quickly and didn't duck soon enough. The result was a gash on his forehead as he hit the top of the door frame. When he got to the house Grandma patched him up by using Mercurochrome, a reddish healing liquid she used for everything short of cancer. It stained Grandpa's forehead red, of course, and the red stayed there for weeks. Big deal. You can work, go to the store, attend church and do lots of other stuff with a red forehead. You just keep moving. You stay focused on your target. You stop don't for the small stuff. And you learn that almost everything bothersome is the small stuff.

Our farm DNA also taught us how things work. We never imagined that food came simply from a supermarket. We knew what the rows of corn looked like and what it took to plant and harvest them even if we ourselves never participated in planting or harvesting (though one hot summer I led a corn detasseling crew at Earl and Mildred Hughes' farm just outside Woodstock). We knew about the sources of milk, of beef, of pork. Maybe we never cut the head off a chicken and watched it run around before collapsing spent, but we watched our grandmothers do that. My Grandma Helander was really good at it, too. We saw generations before us churn their own butter and peel their own apples to make applesauce. We had a visceral grasp of all these processes so we understood that absolutely everything has "some assembly required" signs on it, at least metaphorically, and we knew that meant almost nothing would go right the first time. So we didn't expect perfection and didn't moan in exasperation when we found out — again — that we were right.

The other thing we learned because of our farming background was that it's good to laugh, even when things go wrong. Grandpa Tammeus loved to tell the story of the day he took my little cousin Sally, then about two or three years old, with him to gather eggs from the chicken coop. His mistake was that he gave Sally a metal bucket. And from the other side of the coop Grandpa could hear her tossing the eggs — thud-crack, thud-crack, thud-crack — into the bucket. He just howled with laughter telling that story. He howled every time. And, by the way, we learned to call eggs cackleberries.

We also learned that once you find a good joke to tell, you never give it up. Here was Grandpa Helander's favorite joke: *Three Scots were sitting in church together. When it came time for the collection, one of them fainted and the other two carried him out.* That's it. That's the whole joke, making fun of the alleged cheapness of people from Scotland. I'm sure I heard that joke two hundred times. And each time Grandpa laughed, which of course made everyone else laugh. So even in humor, you keep on keeping on, at least until you discover that the jokes your ancestors told were offensive, as some of them surely were. (Sorry, people with origins in Scotland.)

As we grew up, we also learned that the farm — and life — could be dirty and brutal. You had to handle manure from all kinds of animals. You had to sweat. You had to be isolated and lonely at times. You had to rely on the unreliable weather. Sometimes the rain failed you and your land dried up and blew away. Sometimes it drowned your land. Sometimes the heat burned up your crop. And if you didn't know how to handle all that, you would be in a lot of trouble.

You also had to understand that life was full of death. The very animals farmers raised were destined for death so others might eat and live. Mostly the chickens who laid the eggs didn't get to mother them into life as chicks. Mostly the steers who wandered the fields and ate the grain did it so that they could become hamburger and steaks. When snakes or rats infested a farm, you had to kill them. And the cats in the barn kept down the mice population. That's how life works. Middle Americans know that.

I worry sometimes about how removed a lot of our children and grandchildren have become from the farm. Somehow visiting a zoo doesn't teach the same lessons. Or reading about food production. Or having a pet. You surely don't get farm DNA in your system from playing Farmville on Facebook. And maybe that's another way we Middle Americans have failed those who have come after us. We haven't done very well passing on our farm DNA. And in many ways the nation will be impoverished because of that.

Phones

If you wanted to call my house in Woodstock when I was a small boy, here was our phone number: 893. Some people had numbers even simpler. The Neuchiller family's number was 20. In today's nine-digit ZIP code world, the only time you have just two numbers is if your age or your weight is under a hundred. Well, or your I.Q.

THIS IS A STANDARD WESTERN ELECTRIC 300-SERIES NON-DIAL DESK PHONE USED IN BELL SYSTEM EXCHANGES, SUCH AS IN WOODSTOCK, IN THE 1940s AND '50s. — COURTESY AT&T ARCHIVES AND HISTORY CENTER

Back then you'd just pick up the old black desk phone and an operator would come on and say, "Number, please." Very polite operators we had.

One day I called home from junior high school to get a ride — an unusual request — because I had tons of stuff to carry and the weather was terrible. But the line was busy. So a few minutes later I tried again. Still busy. Then I tried again and again and again until finally the operator said with considerable exasperation in her voice, "Bill, your parents are on the phone. Just *wait* awhile." I had never told the operator who I was. I had simply given her our number. As someone smarter than I am once said, one advantage to living in a small town is that even if you have no idea what you're doing, someone else always does.

In 1958, when my family returned from two years of living in India, our number had changed and grown a digit in length. It became 2770. But that didn't last long. It soon became FEderal-8-2770. That didn't last long, either. It became fully digitized to 338-2770 — until, that is, we had to add the 815 area code. But once the area code, prefix and number were set, my parents kept their same number for 40 or more years — until death did them part from it.

In some ways these changes in our phone systems represented all the technological changes that have buffeted Middle Americans since our birth. In fact, although my phone life started with 893, we were connected to an even earlier generation of phone technology through an even earlier generation of people than our parents. For instance, when I was in grade school I saw a working hand-cranked phone on the wall when we'd visit the farm house where my father grew up in Delavan, Illinois. It was a party line, not a private line. So each party on the line had a special ring. That allowed everyone to know not to pick up when someone was calling the neighbor and not you.

From that archaic beginning we have moved faster and faster all the way to the latest generation of smart phones, which can give you the news, pay your bills, post messages on Facebook, deposit checks and wake you in the morning with gentle sounds of the surf rolling in. And as each new generation of phones has come along old ones have been reduced to scrap or semi-cool paper weights.

And we've adapted to it all — the phones, the faxes, the desktop computers, the laptops, the iPads, the smart phones, the computerized kitchen appliances (and car engines). Yes, of course, some Middle Americans have adapted with complaint, frustration, anger. And some have embraced quickly whatever was fresh, however silly or tiny the change made to the latest version. But we have learned to deal with it, made our accommodations, found our high-tech comfort zones, even added to the stockpile of technology with our own inventions.

It's this adaptive ability I celebrate. It kept us from going crazy when the IRS would issue new tax-filing rules each year, when new cars no longer came with plain old keys, when phone answering machines with cassette tapes gave way to digitized versions we had to figure out how to work, when VCR players on which we finally learned to record TV shows were replaced by something else that required new instructions, when we quit using film in cameras and started storing just-shot pictures on tiny cards not much bigger than a stamp. And on and on and on.

Some of us liked these new toys. Some of us loathed them. But we figured out how to make do, how not to declare ourselves Luddites and retire from the game. We stuck our faces into the winds of change and said, "Bring it on," even when we hoped no one would bring on another change for at least one more week.

And it was this attitude that helped America face the blistering pace of change in the world — the spread of nuclear weapons, the collapse of the British Empire, the decolonization of the world, the fall of the Soviet Union and its hold on satellite nations in Eastern Europe, the rise of violent extremism that relied on distorted versions of Islam for its existence, the chaos in Africa, the Arab Spring (and Winter), the rise of Japan, China and India as major powers, even the recognition that, as someone once said, Brazil is the country of the future and always will be. All of this and more. Sometimes we didn't adapt quickly enough or well enough but we finally always adapted, always found our sea legs.

It makes me want to pick up the phone, wait for "number, please," ask for 893 and tell my long-dead parents that we're making it. I wonder if they'd take a collect call. Remember those?

"*People, people, people*"

CLARENCE OLSON JUNIOR HIGH SCHOOL IN WOODSTOCK NOW IS CLARENCE OLSON ELEMENTARY SCHOOL, AND IT'S WHERE RUTH WILSON TAUGHT ME SUBJECT-VERB-PREDICATE. OR HOWEVER THEY WERE SUPPOSED TO LINE UP.

Ruth Isabelle Wilson, who taught those of us in her Clarence Olson Junior High School eighth grade class to diagram any English sentence it was possible to write, once encouraged me to memorize and recite the whole of the Alfred Lord Tennyson poem, "The Charge of the Light Brigade."

All six verses. All 265 words. All delivered with zest — even power — in front of my classmates, whose appreciation for history and poetry seemed to me to be on a par with their appreciation of the subtleties of the various theories of the atonement or the predictions embedded in eschatology. Even now I cannot say why I allowed Miss Wilson to convince me to honor a poem about a deadly military disaster involving Brits, Cossacks and Russians. Perhaps it was one way Middle Americans learned a bit of world history. Or perhaps it was a way to honor all the teachers who, in so many ways, helped to shape us.

But I do recall the secret thrill I got as I practically yelled out some of the verses, such as *"Cannon to right of them,/Cannon to left of them,/Cannon in front of them/Volley'd and thunder'd"*. Why, there was drama there, action, danger. And if I managed to convey all of that in a believable way, perhaps one or more of the girls in class would find me attractive and perhaps one or more of the boys in the class would be jealous of me for my rhetorical skills.

And maybe I'd get an "A" from Miss Wilson and not disappoint my parents, especially my mother, who sometimes was a substitute English teacher at the high school up the street from our house and who, thus, knew a little something about poetry and the authority of words.

What I do know is that Miss Wilson never forgot my stirring rendition of poetry that grew out of a British attack in the Crimean War in 1854, a mere fifty-three years before Ruth Wilson was born twelve miles up the road from Woodstock in Harvard, Illinois, long a claimant to the title of Milk Capital of the World and site of the still-continuing annual Harvard Milk Days parade and festival.

In her late retirement years, Miss Wilson had moved to the Sunset Apartments in Woodstock and, finally to the adjacent Hearthstone Manor, the assisted living and nursing facility in which both of my parents died, though at the time of their deaths it was called Sunset Manor. When I visited my father there well into his senile dementia in late 1991 I also ran into Ruth Wilson. First thing out of her mouth was her vivid memory of my impressive recitation of "The Charge of the Light Brigade."

It's hard to imagine that my miniscule rhetorical achievement in 1959 could have been a true highlight of her life. In fact, it made me a little sad to realize that might be the case. Was there so little else that competed for her highlight reel from having taught for two years at a rural school, another nineteen years at Belvidere (Illinois) Junior High School and then twenty-four years at Clarence Olson or from having outlived her parents, three brothers and a sister? Or, more likely, was she just deeply attentive to the young lives she was helping to educate — an attentiveness that must, in retrospect, be called what it was, love?

Either way, knowing the effect my recitation apparently had on Miss Wilson, I am more careful now to think about how my actions and words may affect others in ways I have difficulty imagining. Just as I hope she was aware that ever since I spent time in her class, I have remembered — and sometimes even used — her repetitive expression of exasperation at what her charges were doing: "People, people, people," she would sigh, with a hard emphasis on the first syllable of each word. She didn't need to add: "What the hell are you thinking?" We knew that thought was deeply implied in the second or third "people." Saying less sometimes is stronger than saying more. It's the same — I know now — with writing.

I also know that we Middle Americans owe a great deal to the teachers who guided us through childhood, implanting within our souls codes of conduct that sought to make us kind, generous, a little chivalrous and certainly curious. We were not and are not always all those things, but the arc of our history bends toward decency. And the Ruth Wilsons, the Joann Steinkes, the Bud Swartouts, the Bill Deans, the Jean Schmiedeskamps and the Jeanette Burbanks in our lives helped to start us on that journey.

Old Themes

FOR FOUR YEARS I WALKED THROUGH THESE DOORS TO ATTEND HIGH SCHOOL AND, SOMETIMES, TO TURN IN
THEMES OF WHICH I WAS OCCASIONALLY PROUD AND OCCASIONALLY NOT.

I can't tell you why, but in the pile of things I retrieved from my parents' house before it was sold in
1996 were examples of some of my high school writings.

One is dated September 20, 1960, written at the start of my sophomore year for English 2A. As
I recall, English (and maybe other) classes were divided — A, B and C — according to the perceived
scholarly wherewithal of the students. In other words, we were tracked, as they said then. As part of
the allegedly elite "A" group of clearly or at least potentially brilliant sophomores (surely the words "elite"
and "sophomores" should never be used in the same sentence), I produced a one-and-a-half-page theme
called, "ENGLISH IS FOR YOU AND FOR NOW." The surprise is that I did not, after that screaming
headline, add the words, "DAMN IT."

Here's part of one of my sentences: "...it is rediculous (sic) for us not to like or care about even one language, are (sic) own!" Only two misspellings there, plus the question of how "like" and "care about" may be different. This effort earned me a B+, even though the teacher noticed and corrected those (and other) errors.

Two years later, in senior English, I gave birth to a twenty-page essay entirely devoted to T.S. Eliot's classic poem, "The Love Song of J. Alfred Prufrock." As I read my paper today I can see all kinds of ways to improve it. And yet what astonishes me is the progress I seem to have made in two years as a writer.

In the Prufrock essay — at least in the ungraded draft I have — there are, for sure, typos and editing marks made necessary by errant typewriter strikes. But the content is beginning to approach something in the suburbs of maturity, at least for a teen-ager. On page 11, for instance, I write, "Certainly, despair is an incoherent emotion." Now there's a conclusion that all by itself could take a twenty-page essay to unpack. Plus there are footnotes galore. I recall going to the public library in Elgin, Illinois, twenty-five miles from Woodstock, to take advantage of a larger collection of books of criticism to research this Eliot poem. And I obviously found a fair amount to quote.

The question now is what happened between my sophomore and senior years in our nearly all-white, small Midwestern town that allowed me to grow in my writing skills so noticeably? One answer is that I discovered — or at least affirmed — how much I loved to read, and in that process I learned about the power of words. They could make me laugh, cry, shudder. They could change my mind. They even could lead me astray.

For instance, a passage I read in this period from W. Somerset Maugham's *Of Human Bondage*[15] drew me toward atheism for a time. Here it is: "Thinking of Cronshaw, Philip remembered the Persian rug which he had given him, telling him that it offered an answer to his question upon the meaning of life; and suddenly the answer occurred to him: he chuckled: now that he had it, it was like one of the puzzles which you worry over till you are shown the solution and then cannot imagine how it could ever have escaped you. The answer was obvious. Life had no meaning. On the earth, satellite of a star speeding through space, living things had arisen under the influence of conditions which were part of the planet's history; and as there had been a beginning of life upon it so, under the influence of other conditions, there would be an end: man, no more significant than other forms of life, had come not as the climax of creation but as a physical reaction to the environment."

To my sophomoric mind, this was as full and accurate an explanation as I ever could hope to find — even if it ran against the grain of everything I had been taught until I read this passage. I had been not exactly born again but more like unborn again. Eventually, however, I had enough lapses of disbelief that I gave it up, having found my attraction to atheism to be quite destructive of my relations with people who, I thought then, were not as astute as I was and who continued in their foolish commitment to superstition and myth.

Words, in other words, mattered, I learned, as did the ideas they were used to convey. And I was determined to learn enough about words to be able to affect others with my own employment of them.

One of the things that led me in the right direction as this process was occurring was that I was introduced to some terrific poetry as well as prose. I can't imagine what might have become of me had I been stuck just with the cloying verses of, say, Helen Steiner Rice or Rod McEwen. Would I have sing-songed and clichéd my way through a writing life? I've committed enough of those felonies as it is, no doubt. But at least I had better models. At least I got to know of Eliot and Auden, Moore and Yeats, Stevens and Jarrell, among many others. And at least I knew enough to let those writers influence me instead of the shallow silliness one so often finds in homemade poetry by church ladies, God love 'em.

Even in an insular town like Woodstock in the 1950s and '60s — where teens were marinating in a pop culture that offered endless rock 'n' roll on WLS radio in Chicago and the illusion that hot cars with rumbling exhaust systems made you a worthy human being — some of us were subverting the conventional wisdom by finding examples of extraordinary writing, world-class music, classic theater, museum-quality art. We did not talk about this in the hallways of our schools or in the cars we drove relentlessly around The Square. But we were subversives, nonetheless. And in the end it freed us, just as similar discoveries also freed many other Middle Americans around the country.

It may be foolish to preserve high school writings if one wishes to imagine himself a prodigy at that age. But I hang on to this stuff partly because it reminds me how hard good writing is, how what is written without difficulty is read without joy, how writers must write and write and write just to avoid getting worse, how *rediculous* it is for us not to like or care about even one language, *are* own!

Romance

JANET BATES (LEFT) WAS MY GIRLFRIEND IN SEVENTH AND PART OF EIGHTH GRADE UNTIL SHE FELL FOR AN OLDER GUY. BECKY BLOCKSOM (RIGHT) AND I WENT STEADY AS FRESHMEN. BOTH GIRLS GOT OVER ME WITHOUT MUCH TROUBLE.

"I think it would be best for both of us if you would just forget that I even exist. Why don't you just try it. I bet it sure wouldn't be very hard." — Part of a note from my girlfriend, Cherry Hunt, (a freshman) dumping me when I was a senior in high school.

It started in kindergarten at Dean Street School. I fell in love with Carol Harrington, who sat opposite me in the big circle of five-year-olds who made up Lila Dobbs' class of small scholars.

In turn, Peggy Dittman fell in love with me. I knew this because she would sit cross-legged across from me, not far from Carol, and purposefully give me flashes of her panties and beyond. Besides that, she followed me home a couple of times.

As we moved through the grades, my loves changed from Carol to Kathy to Linda to Sharon — some of whom never knew they were my girlfriends, given that we had no approved protocols for love at that age. All we knew is that something stirred our hearts.

But this early experience of being wildly attracted to someone of the opposite sex later helped many of us understand that homosexuality is an orientation, not a choice, and that we heterosexuals could not name a time when we *chose* to be straight. What would I have done had I discovered as a kindergartener that it was not Carol Harrington but Roger Knuth who made my heart race?

I have no idea, and yet later we learned that some of our schoolmates were having those same-sex emotional experiences (not Roger, by the way, may he rest in peace) and having to come to terms with feelings that must have struck them as weird and extraordinary.

It has taken Middle Americans decades to accommodate the idea that homosexuality is an unusual but perfectly normal sexual orientation that has existed among human beings for as long as anyone knows. Before we could get there, however, we had to fight through the false certitude of Bible teachers who misread scripture and who swore that God would send gays and lesbians to hell. I won't give you my longish answer to such biblical nonsense here, but you can find it on my daily "Faith Matters" blog at http://bit.ly/q0T102.

Part of what we males had to do to figure all of this out was to go back and remember our Carol Harringtons, our Kathy Nelsons, our Linda Laings — those females who, we imagined, wanted to be with us and love us day and night for the rest of our lives, even if we had no clear idea what love would look like or the kind of commitment we were seeking and offering. When we did that we understood that those of us who are heterosexual had no choice in the matter. As males, our only choice was whether to ask Janet Bates (or some other girl) to dance with us at the noon dances in seventh grade at Clarence Olson Junior High or to let our shyness keep us seated. The debate wasn't between asking Janet Bates or asking Ted Krueger, who himself was trying to get up the courage to ask some other girl.

The rituals of dating began in junior high, though mostly they were limited to the noon dances, a party at someone's house or meeting someone at the Miller Theater for a movie. And although high school proved to be a time of sexual contact and experimentation for some of our schoolmates, many of us — though several times intensely in love — remained virgins until at least college if not all the way until we were married. The most exciting thing beyond masturbation that we boys did sexually was to find a quiet place to park with our girlfriends and neck, as we called it. And sometimes we never made it much below the neck.

Mostly we were unguided sexual missiles. I didn't know for sure how babies were made until I was into my teen-age years, and I was not alone, despite the boasts of boys in the locker room. Most of our parents didn't bother to give us "the talk," figuring, I suppose, that by the time we needed to know about sex we'd have picked it up by osmosis. Which we sort of did, along with plenty of misinformation. Indeed, it wasn't until well into the women's liberation movement of the 1960s and '70s that some women of our generation of Middle Americans learned how their own bodies worked. You cannot be free, independent, autonomous if you don't know that. (And maybe that was the point of ignorance.)

In junior high and high school there were all kinds of signs and signals to alert others to your relationship status. An upside-down decorative buckle on the back of a pair of khaki pants, for instance, was an indication that a boy was taken. And when boys gave girls a class or friendship ring of some kind, the girls would wrap it with angora fur or something similar to set it off so no one could miss her relationship status.

I gave Becky Blocksom a "going steady" ring when we were freshmen in high school, and much of the time that she had it she wore it on a chain around her neck, perhaps partly to keep her parents from knowing she had it by slipping it inside her blouse — a destination I myself never reached. By the end of the school year Becky gave me back the ring, having decided we had no future.

As we stumbled along in these relationships we began to understand that long-term commitments require lots of work and could not be sustained on the fuel of lust. And although we grasped that concept intellectually, we found it hard to sustain in our later married lives. Oh, some Middle Americans followed the pattern set by their parents — long marriages no matter what, even if neither husband nor wife eventually felt (or did) anything for each other that might be called love. But lots of us also contributed to the rising divorce rate — even when, as was the case with my first marriage, we (well, in my case, I) didn't want to let go of what we had. My wife entered into a second relationship before fixing or ending her marriage to me. As one who takes commitments seriously — especially one entered into "before God and these witnesses" — I found this one of the most painful experiences of my life, particularly because the man with whom she was having an affair was our pastor, whom I had helped to bring to our church in my role as a member of the pastor search committee. It was an outrageous betrayal on the part of both of them, though, of course, no marriage falls apart without contributions from both spouses.

Having grown up in a mid-century culture that seemed to view divorce as a moral failure, I found it hard to accept the reality that although I certainly contributed to the failure of my marriage, in the end her choice to have an affair was much more about her than it was about me. I suppose if we Middle Americans had seen some more models of marital honesty, including reconciliation when things broke, we might have been better at holding our own marriages together. But we all knew that many of the marriages we observed were unhappy, held together with bailing wire, chewing gum and maybe duct tape. And like olives out of a tightly packed bottle, divorces became easier to get and to stomach once the first one had happened.

A few years ago I found a stack of letters that my girlfriend had written to me in my first year in college, when she still was a senior in high school. Our love did not survive that separation, but all those years later I was struck by her occasional words expressing a desire for me to be with her. These words were scattered among lots of mundane silliness about what was happening to her in school or with her friends or family, but just to read again and remember that as teen-agers we were sorting out our mysterious feelings of attraction and attractiveness took me back to an innocent time when we were discovering that nothing is more powerful than love.

We Middle Americans, as I say, know that about love intellectually and some of us know it deep in our souls. But the hard work of love often has thrown us off track, moving us away from its purity, its necessity, its essential nature as we have turned instead to what inevitably turns out to be inadequate substitutes for its essence.

We sometimes think this: If only we could start over, holding each other closely and slow-dancing over the lunch hour in junior high to "Smoke Gets in Your Eyes" or "Earth Angel." Oh, if only. But then we get over it and are grateful for the love in front of us.

On Learning Courage

MY BOYHOOD FRIEND TOM NEVILLE, WHO DIED OF LEUKEMIA WHEN WE WERE SOPHOMORES IN HIGH SCHOOL, IS BURIED IN MCHENRY COUNTY MEMORIAL PARK CEMETERY IN WOODSTOCK. I WAS ONE OF HIS PALLBEARERS.

Long before we buried him on that arctic day, before leukemia had battered his young body, I remember Tom Neville raising his hand in class. Raising it all alone. It was in fifth grade, I think, at Dean Street School.

The teacher — Jeanette Burbank, if I'm right about the year — had asked the class a question about whatever we were studying: "How many of you think the answer is (blank)?" A bunch of hands went up, followed by more and more as people began to sense the landslide. Finally, every hand but Tom's was up, mine included.

"Now how many of you think the answer is (blank)?" And there was Tom. He was not hesitant, but neither was he ram-rod anxious to be noticed. He just raised his hand. And he kept it up to be sure Miss Burbank saw his vote.

It was, in retrospect, an enormously courageous act for a child. Tom was willing to be different, to be an oddball, to be singled out for ridicule. But, Miss Burbank told us, Tom was the only one who got the answer right. He might be different, a nonconformist in this case, but he should be singled out for praise, not ridicule.

I loved Tom for that. I disliked myself, of course, for going along with the crowd on the answer — an answer I wasn't sure about. But the more I thought about it then and even years later, the more I was so proud of Tom that I could have cried.

I did cry just before Tom died. It was January of 1961, our sophomore year in high school, and Tom was in the hospital for the last time. I walked into his room, where his mother was at his bedside. He looked swollen, tired, defeated, reddened somehow even in the dim light. It had been some weeks since I had seen him, and I was unprepared, at age sixteen (Tom had turned fifteen the previous October 1), to see someone my age being biologically destroyed.

I spoke to Tom that day about stupid things. I told him I'd just gotten my learner's permit for driver's education class, having turned sixteen on January 18 — as if Tom either cared or as if he ever would get the chance to drive himself. Within a few days, on January 30, Tom died. We collected ourselves — I was one of the pallbearers — at 2 p.m. on Thursday, February 2 (Groundhog Day, later a special Woodstock holiday), at the First Methodist Church on West South Street, a few blocks down the street from my house, and said farewell in a painful, awkward way.

What did we know? We had no idea how to bury someone our age, how to celebrate his brief life, how to mourn, how to imagine mortality for ourselves. Oh, we had already has some earlier experiences with the death of someone our own age in grade school when a classmate was accidentally shot and killed by his brother while hunting. But because that's all we learned about what happened and because I never went to his funeral, the experience taught me and my friends virtually nothing about people our own age dying. We whispered about that grade-school death but soon we set it aside and got on with life.[16]

But Tom, like us, was growing toward adulthood. He started high school with us, seemingly well. Then he missed school, returned, missed more, returned. Some of my friends and I went to his house to spend time with him after school now and then when he wasn't well enough to attend school. We wanted him to recover. Mostly we wanted not to be him. Then after a time he couldn't fight this stuff any more. He was out of energy, out of breath, out of options.

So we gathered at the church and, afterward, carried his casket to the hearse and got into cars to ride out to McHenry County Memorial Park Cemetery at the edge of town on a day so cold that it hurt our eyes to stare through the wind into the distance. Somehow we carried Tom's casket to the burial site and listened to whatever final words had to be said by the wonderful pastor, Clarence F. Kerr, a Baptist who became the youth director at my Presbyterian congregation. Then we hurried back to the warmth of the cars, brutalized by both weather and death.

All these years later I have forgiven Tom for dying in the midst of a bleak midwinter, forgiven him for exposing our own mortality. What I now know about Thomas Kenneth Neville is that he taught me courage, taught me not to be afraid to be right when everyone else is wrong, taught me humility about being right. And lots of Middle Americans had someone — child or adult — to impart similar lessons, because many of us have lived out those values in countless ways.

So today whenever I raise my hand to respond to any question or even to ask a question, I remember Tom's hand in the air. I think about how many more times in life — if only he'd had a chance — he would have been right, maybe when the rest of us were wrong. And his absence still makes me angry.

The Unusuals

MY STEPSON CHRIS HAS A SEIZURE DISORDER AND MENTAL RETARDATION, BUT WOULD LIKE TO GIVE EVERYONE IN THE WORLD A HUG. HERE WE'RE PUTTING AWAY A PUZZLE HE JUST FINISHED.

Given the range of what can be expected in any collection of human beings, a town of 7,192 people[17] is inevitably going to contain some citizens who are a little out of the ordinary. When I was a boy Woodstock was home to several such folks. And thank goodness for that. Their presence allowed us Middle Americans (eventually) to understand that life is not homogenous, not all white bread, not all predictable.

Their presence also gave us kids lots of opportunities to be cruel, but it wasn't until we were adults and reflected on this part of life that we recognized the extent of our malice.

There were, first, the mentally and developmentally disabled. Earl, for instance, who was a couple of years older than me, rode his bike all over town in what appeared to be a wild and random pattern of just going and going and going. When I first noticed the disheveled and untethered young man, other kids told me that something was eating Earl's brain and that if we got too close to him we might catch whatever this pernicious disease was.

Though Earl obviously had mental challenges, I later concluded that something had been eating the brains of the kids who said that — something called hatred, prejudice. But when I was an eight- or ten-year-old boy the story of something eating Earl's brain seemed to be plausible. So I did my best to scoot away whenever Earl got close.

Except for the fact that Earl then was much more mobile than my special-needs stepson Chris is now (Chris has a seizure disorder and functions cognitively and socially as roughly a five-year-old) Earl was quite like Chris. At least I now imagine Earl that way. And Chris is the happiest human being I've ever met. If he could, he'd give everyone in the world a hug — and mean it.

But because of cruelty by children, me included, Earl didn't get the chances he should have had to be in relationship with his peers. It's painful to think about even all these years later. Regrets? We Middle Americans have a few.

Another pedal-mobile unusual person in our lives then was Bill Cowlin. He had some kind of neuromuscular disorder — perhaps cerebral palsy — that caused him to walk and speak with great difficulty. Bill had an adult tricycle with a container on the back out of which he'd sell stuff like Fuller brush and Watkins products, plus cards, magazines and wrapping paper as he traveled the Woodstock neighborhoods.

His speech, as I say, was slurred and difficult to grasp, especially for children. Unlike the way we treated Earl, however, we seemed simply to ignore Bill or just politely acknowledge his presence when he was around us. No doubt we made fun of him when he wasn't looking but I don't recall us being cruel to him in front of him, though David Strohm, who grew up near me, remembers doing exactly that, and you can hear his moving story about that at http://www.boomkids.com/transfers/Trust.mp3.

Bill's presence was a lesson in the reality that the human body, however fearfully and wonderfully made, as the Bible says, is also vulnerable to disease and injury and, in the end, cannot be counted on completely to carry us through life. So we Middle Americans have tended to take seriously the idea that we are to care for our bodies. Some of us who are Christian have even repeated the idea that our bodies are the temple of the Holy Spirit, giving us a sacred obligation to care for that temple as if it really mattered.

Well, the truth is that over time we began to forget the lesson about caring for our bodies. Lots of Middle Americans eventually got all out of shape and obese as we consumed processed foods full of trans-fats, sugars and additives that inflamed our arteries. This often reflected a negligence that was hard to explain in a culture that worshiped thinness and fitness and the air-brushed or Photoshopped beauty found in the more elegant magazines.

No doubt some of our neglect of our bodies had to do with the passivity that our relentless and destructive search for constant entertainment encouraged. How else to explain all the ridiculous game, reality and comedy TV shows that somehow find an audience to whom to sell soap or Viagra or sugary carbonated drinks? I'm not sure quite how so many Middle Americans lost their way in this matter, but many did, and our children and grandchildren — also facing an obesity crisis — are suffering for it now, too.

There were others in Woodstock who rambled outside the boundaries of sanity and health, including the pastor of our church, who wound up needing to be a patient at a mental facility in Chicago for a time. And I remember that the son of a dentist had legs crippled by polio or some similar malady. He tottered around — bravely, I always thought — on crutches strapped to each arm. There was nothing mentally amiss about this young man, but to watch him move along a sidewalk was sometimes painful.

So we came to understand that normality was wider than some of us originally thought. It could — and did — include the developmentally, physically and mentally disabled. And we had to account for all that in the way we did life. The result was that eventually, when a kid with mental issues came around or when an old man with the funny name of Frank Pugh (pronounced Pew) from around the corner walked past our house, we quit laughing or making fun and tried to accommodate the reality of abnormality into our idea of normality.

Sometimes it was a rough fit, and we Middle Americans no doubt owe lots of people apologies for our nincompoop responses to them. But as we grew older we understood that everyone — everyone, including us — comes from what department stores sometimes used to call the "Irregular Bin."

All-America City

❖

"THE BIG QUESTION IS NOT WHETHER WE WON AT DETROIT — IT IS, 'WHERE DO WE GO FROM HERE?' "
—John Strohm, December 5, 1963.

THE

CHALLENGE

BEFORE

US

OFFICIAL PRESENTATION DINNER
presented by Woodstock Chamber of Commerce
at Woodstock, Illinois
receives its All-America City Award
from National Municipal League and Look Magazine
Thursday, April 16, 1964

THIS IS THE COVER OF THE PROGRAM FOR THE DINNER AT WHICH THE ALL-AMERICA CITY
AWARD WAS PRESENTED.

A committee of Woodstock big shots went to Detroit in early December 1963 to make a presentation to a panel of folks who would select that year's winners of the National Municipal League's "All-America City" awards.

A few weeks later I came home from my freshman year of college for Christmas vacation, arriving by train late on a snowy night way past the time when people in my house were expecting me. I wasn't all that keen to walk — with luggage — the half mile or so home through the storm or to call my folks that late. So I was happy to see a police car sitting in the train station parking lot. I conned the cop at the wheel, Frank Beau, into giving me a ride to 415 West South Street.

I'd just settled into the back seat when Frank told me it would be a few minutes before we left because he was waiting for a copy of *The Chicago Tribune*, which was arriving on the same train that brought me home. Eventually he got out of his car, picked up a *Trib* and got back in. He flipped a few pages until he declared, "Yep, there it is." I asked what. He said it was a story saying that Woodstock had just been named an All-America City. He seemed quite proud and happy but I didn't know what to think. My reflexive teen-age mind immediately came up with this: *What? People outside of Woodstock think Woodstock is something special? What do they know?*

The Woodstock committee, headed by my parents' good friend John Strohm, had focused on what it called its "eight points" — "a safer city," "more jobs," "better health," "better education," "more fun," "expanded culture," "better living" and "better people."

The idea of "better people" amused me even back then. I know that organizers meant to suggest that our citizens were well educated, thoughtful, friendly, reliable and possessive of many similar virtues. But the phrase struck me then — and strikes me now — as arrogant and bearing a faint whiff of eugenics, that pseudo-science about human engineering that the Nazis loved so much. As I say, the organizers didn't have anything like that in mind when they used that phrase, but surely they could have avoided such an implication through better wording chosen by some of Woodstock's "better people."

In my *Kansas City Star* column I once noted that no one speaks more nostalgically or lovingly about a hometown than the people who have left it. And, of course, this is because they tend to erase the memories of those events or people that caused them to depart, remembering mostly the good times and good people. Selective memory is part of human nature. But as someone who in 1963 had already left Woodstock in my spirit (even if my permanent address would remain there throughout my out-of-state college years), I still was close enough to know in some detail what was wrong with my hometown — knowledge that made it hard to accept the idea that we were being honored as an All-America City.

I knew, for instance, in the way that teen-agers are certain of things, that my high school seemed pretty much geared to C students, with a few exceptions. (Today, by contrast, it's rated among the top high schools in the nation.) And I knew that my church included hypocrites — people who on Sundays pledged allegiance to a moral way of life but who seemed unable to live up to their pledge during the week. I knew that among the adults in town there was adultery, illegal gambling in private clubs and other moral failings. (It took me another dozen years after high school to acknowledge that I was among the hypocrites who needed to be in church because, at its best, it's a first-aid station for sinners not a museum for saints. Church is, at its best, a community of screw-ups.[18])

So this national honor for my hometown helped me to develop a necessarily nuanced way of thinking about the world around me. I could be proud and grateful for the All-America honor while also being honest about the reality on the ground — a reality captured decade after decade in photos and words by local p.r. man and journalist Don Peasley, a community treasure and friend of my parents and me. Don died at age 90 in 2013.[19]

For many reasons, this ability to be both a patriot and a critic seems not terribly unusual among Middle Americans. And it did not spring forth just from the experience of the Vietnam War, though in that matter we learned to try to support our troops even when questioning the morality of the war itself and, by implication, the morality of anyone who would agree to fight in it. But Vietnam surely was an example of a situation in which we Middle Americans learned that giving ourselves over one hundred percent to some cause was probably silly given that if human beings were involved in the cause something would be amiss.

So most Middle Americans are not people Eric Hoffer called (in his book of this title) *The True Believer*, who turn over the keys to their brains to leaders of one cause or another. Rather, we know that our most cherished idols have feet of clay, that our heroes have dark sides, that even Mother Teresa wondered if God was paying any attention and that we ourselves are capable of both astonishing good and immense evil. Oh, sometimes we fall into the trap of politicians who want to tell us that the world is black and white, that we are the good guys and someone else is the "evil-doer." But in our bones, our marrow, our soul we know that life is more complicated than that.

It's this sense of moderation, of lack of extremism, of being in the broad middle that has characterized most Middle Americans. And it is the characteristic we now find under severe threat, as one ideologue after another stakes out an uncompromising position. We wish we knew how to stem that tide of rigidity. All we know is that if it keeps up America will become dysfunctional in countless ways and all but ungovernable. And the failure would be laid partly (and rightly) at our feet for not being smart or persuasive enough to stop it.

Mobility

My father, a central Illinois farm boy, got around — at least once thanks to Air Canada. Notice the "Expo '67" logo on the plane. I attended that world's fair in Montreal that year, but without Dad.

I've visited Egypt's pyramids twice — once as a boy and once as an adult. When this photo was taken I was on a post-9/11 trip to Saudi Arabia, Egypt and Uzbekistan in 2002 with other journalists.

We cut across country to Norris City & Norris Dam (in Tennessee), *a mammoth project. Government also carries on fish hatcheries near the dam. Norris City is a pretty little town with nearly all new houses. At the dam we first noticed separate drinking fountains for colored & white folks.* — From the June 11, 1939, entry in my mother's diary of a road trip she and Dad took from Illinois to Indiana, Kentucky, Tennessee, North Carolina and Georgia.

To visit my maternal grandparents when I was a boy we had to load up the car and drive a hundred miles south to Streator, Illinois. A visit to my paternal grandparents required almost a hundred miles beyond Streator to get to Delavan, Illinois.

The great modern Middle American mobility parade — which acknowledges but does not include the pioneers and their Conestoga wagons — already had begun in my parents' generation. My generation made mobility such a common occurrence that I'm surprised any of us ever put down roots. But many of us finally learned to balance roots and wings and to appreciate both. And many Middle Americans, though well-traveled, have been pretty consistent about finding home base and sticking to it.

My own family probably was not unusual in its wanderlust and the creative tension that characteristic has in relation to the desire for permanence. Except for the two years that my parents lived with us in India, they always called Illinois their home. Oh, they moved a bit after college and marriage to the small Illinois towns of Shelbyville and Greenville, but when they made it to Woodstock in the mid-1940s, it was their permanent home until death.

My sisters and I, however, wound up scattered from coast to coast — Berkeley, California (Karin), to Kansas City, Missouri (me), to Libertyville, Illinois (Mary), to Durham, North Carolina, (with a summer home on Cape Cod — Barbara). I've voted in Illinois, New York, Kansas and Missouri. Two of my siblings also have lived for a time in Texas. And we've traveled a lot. I've been in about thirty-five countries, for instance, and Karin once lived in Florence, Italy, for well over a year.

When it came time to find people for my high school graduation class's fifty-year reunion in 2013, I noted that there was a core of our approximately 120 classmates who never left (or left and returned to) Woodstock. But we also had classmates living in Michigan, Tennessee, Texas, Minnesota, Wisconsin, Arizona, Hawaii, Alaska and other places. It was in our era, after all, that rapid travel and quick relocation became not just possible but eventually even expected. The Conestoga wagons had given way to railroads, then to automobiles, then airplanes. And we who are grandchildren and great-grandchildren of people who came to our shores by ship (some in chains) quickly adapted to the new modes of transportation.

We are, after all, residents of a pasted-together land that sometimes seems far too big for its own good. Many of the small early states of New England mimicked the packed-together geography of Europe, but as the frontier moved west, the size of the states began to grow and eventually it was important to travel if somehow this patchwork quilt of a country was to hold itself together in any meaningful political or cultural way. Worldwide, airlines carried 2.8 billion passengers in 2011 and that number is expected to rise to 3.6 billion by 2016.[20] In 2012, more than 642 million passengers flew within the U.S.[21]

We get around.

My own family's history of getting around in major ways can be traced to a 1955 road trip to the West Coast that my parents thought would be our last opportunity to travel together as a family, partly because my oldest sister, Karin, would be graduating from high school the next year. So on Monday, June 13, 1955, we packed up our midnight-blue 1952 Packard for a 10 a.m. departure that finally got under way about 2:30 p.m. as a light drizzle began.

We would be on the road — my parents, my three sisters and I — for three weeks covering 6,100 miles. Our first stop was Ulysses S. Grant's home in Galena, Illinois. Then we went to a wedding in Iowa, visited relatives in Nebraska, saw the Rockies in Colorado, spent a night at Zion National Park in Utah, had breakfast early one morning in Las Vegas (where my sister Barbara illegally hit a small jackpot of nickels from a slot machine), and finally visited various family friends in California before returning through Salt Lake City, Wyoming, the Black Hills of South Dakota and Rochester, Minnesota, home of the Mayo

Clinic, where Barbara had had five operations for a hair lip and cleft palate and where my mother wrote a small booklet introducing people to Mayo and Rochester.

But less than a year later this 1955 trip would seem like a simple and brief undertaking by comparison to our 1956 move to India, where we lived for almost two years so my father could be part of a University of Illinois agriculture team.

In many ways, I have been a traveler ever since then, and although I may have traveled more than many Middle Americans because I'm a journalist, I'm certainly not unique among Middle Americans, whose travel for work and pleasure has helped them gain a broader vision of humanity that was not nearly as possible for their ancestors.

Mobility has allowed us Middle Americans to be more comfortable with people whose ethnic, religious, economic and social backgrounds differ from ours. And yet deep within the Middle American psyche is a longing for the stability of home. So for many of us the pattern is that we live in one place for a long time but from that place we travel a lot. As I say, my travel experience as a journalist is a little out of the ordinary, but it somehow doesn't seem to me that I'm an outlier just because I've datelined out of more than two hundred and fifty different cities (Abiquiu, New Mexico, to Woodward, Oklahoma, Aix-en-Provence, France, to Woodstock, Vermont, not to mention Bukhara, Uzbekistan, and Safed, Israel). And yet I've called Kansas City my home for most of fifty years.

Our lives as travelers have stretched from the days when all airliners were driven by propellers to the modern jet era, which has turned into an uncomfortable hassle as post-9/11 security requirements have forced us through long, slow lines and as a deregulated airline industry has begun charging extra for almost everything, from checked baggage to on-board snacks. And yet, in our Middle American way, we have adapted, made our accommodations and continued to move about the country and the world.

I've often been struck in my travels with the reality that people from the Midwest visiting the coasts typically are thought of as parochial, but it's the folks on the coasts who haven't been to the Midwest, who don't know that the much larger of the two cities named Kansas City is in Missouri, who can't name a single city in Nebraska, who consider everything west of Pittsburgh and east of Las Vegas as just fly-over country where nothing much happens. As I write this chapter in late 2013, I've already been just this year to Washington state and British Columbia, to Colorado, Vermont, New Hampshire, Massachusetts, Connecticut, Iowa and Illinois, to say nothing of Kansas, to which I can walk in about fifteen minutes. And, as I say, this is not a crazily untypical Middle American travel schedule.

Still, in our fantasy lives, we long for what Kurt Vonnegut once dreamed up for travel — to move from place to place immediately by being "transinfundibulated." But we worry that the transinfundibulation companies will lose our luggage, too.

Membership

‹——◆——›

WILLIAM DAVID TAMMEUS

Boys' State, 3; Student Council, 2, 3, Vice-president, 4; Class Vice-president, 1; WOODCOHI, 4; LE-PRO-CON, 3, 4, Sports Editor, 2; Football Trainer, 2, 3, 4; Basketball, 1, 2, 4; Pep Club, 1, 2; F.T.A., 4; French Club, 3; Science Club, 3; Band, 1, 2, 3, 4; Orchestra, 1, 2, 3, 4; Madison Scholarship, 3; Music Contest, 1, 2, 3, 4; Speech Contest, 1, 2, 4; Thespians, 1, 2, 4, President, 3; Choir, 1, 2; National Honor Society, 3, President, 4 United Nations Trip, 3; The Wizard of Oz; Finian's Rainbow; Time Out for Ginger.

THIS IS MY SENIOR ENTRY IN THE 1963 *WOODCOHI*, MY WOODSTOCK COMMUNITY HIGH SCHOOL YEARBOOK. LIKE MANY MIDDLE AMERICANS, I HAVE BEEN A JOINER.

"I guess I wouldn't be happy if I weren't involved in everything going on..." — A comment from my mother in an April 19, 1970, letter, after listing all the meetings and events she had attended the previous week.

"Sunday noon we will have dinner at the church and then attend the annual meeting. Monday night is Welcome Wagon Club. Tuesday night we attend the annual dinner meeting of Memorial Hospital. Wednesday night we go to Martinetti's for the annual dinner meeting of the Mental Health Assn. Friday night is CWU (Church Women United) annual meeting." — In a January 20, 1972, letter from my mother.

"This is a big day for Dad. His beloved Kiwanis club has been falling apart this past year. Dad finally talked them into changing the time of meeting from night to noon. They will also leave the Moose Lodge and meet in the Woodstock Mall. I can't wait to have him come home and tell me all about it. . .Dad just came in. They had 21 at the meeting. School Supt. spoke. Food was good, so I think they are on their way to new life. Hope so." — In a July 5, 1989, letter to my family from my mother.

Middle Americans have been joiners. Start an organization and Middle Americans will sign up to be part of it. Well, except, of course, for extremists groups like al-Qaida or the Ku Klux Klan. As soon as Middle Americans hit "like" on the Facebook page of such radical groups, they're no longer Middle Americans.

Middle American have joined the Kiwanis, the Rotary, the Lions, Elks, Optimists or Moose clubs, the Veterans of Foreign Wars, garden clubs, the American Legion, quilting circles, Bible study groups and, in Woodstock, the Seneca Ladies Literary Society, which started in April 1855 as the Franklinville Ladies Literary Society, Franklinville being a small rural community a few miles outside of town. They joined investment clubs, country clubs and the Chamber of Commerce. They joined high school sports booster clubs, the PTA and alumni associations. This joining tendency starts early, too, with the Cub Scouts and Campfire Girls, the 4-H Club and the church's junior choir.

One benefit offered by many of these organizations is that they give out awards to encourage good citizenship and in the process give members a bit of local fame. For instance, as I write this, I'm looking at a list of Woodstock "Lions Club Citizens of the Year." The list starts in 1947 with Clarence Olson, the band leader and teacher after whom my junior high school was named. The list includes Emery "Tiny" Hansman, Woodstock's chief of police when I grew up; Harold Beth, a banker; John Strohm, a journalist and author and on and on.

I'm also looking at the words next to my senior picture in the *Woodcohi* high school yearbook, words that list my extracurricular activities over four years. Apparently I joined almost everything that would have me. I was a class officer and a member of the student council. I joined the yearbook staff and the newspaper staff. I joined the basketball team and was the football team's trainer. I was a member of Thespians, the band, the orchestra, the choir, the French Club, the Science Club, the Future Teachers of America and the National Honor Society. (How did I miss Latin Club?) And the list didn't include non-school groups to which I belonged, such as DeMolay and the church youth group.

As my generation has moved toward senescence, we have noticed that although our children and grandchildren are busy people, they're not the joiners our generation of Middle Americans has been. Certainly as our children have become adults they have not flocked to Rotary or Kiwanis clubs, haven't committed to be church members in the way their parents and grandparents have, haven't seemed to need the social contact these various organizations provided to us in many ways. Instead, they often have found something like community in cyberspace. Probably they have hit "like" on the Facebook pages of many more organizations than we ever joined, but liking a page has not meant showing up at 7 p.m. every other Tuesday for a meeting.

Membership in all these organizations taught Middle Americans — or at least reinforced previous lessons about — dependability, commitment, organization, purpose. We know Robert's Rules of Order. We know how to create an agenda. And we know what constitutes a quorum. All this was a structure that allowed us to accomplish things that we believed were worth accomplishing.

Some of this still is valuable but much of what used to happen in the groups we joined now happens in other ways — ways that are neither better nor worse (though sometimes more efficient), simply different. We connect through Facebook and Twitter to organize everything from a gathering of friends for dinner to Arab Spring revolutions. And membership today is much more fluid, with people coming and going on an ad hoc basis more frequently than was our experience decades ago.

Only later in our lives did some Middle Americans start bowling alone[22], as the title of a book by Robert D. Putnam has it. Oh, of course, there have always been a few loners in our midst, some people too shy, too lacking in confidence, too emotionally damaged to sustain membership in any group. But on the whole we're the folks who have made our neighborhood associations hum, our classic car clubs succeed. We have found birds of our feathers and flocked together in ways that have not simply entertained us or filled our otherwise-empty hours but in ways that also have brought education and community, opportunity and enhancement to the places in which we have lived.

Our commitment to membership, in fact, sometimes has meant that we haven't been discerning about when to let an organization die. For instance, congregations that used to boast large memberships sometimes now dwindle to a few dozen people who simply cannot abide the idea of merging with another congregation or dissolving altogether. I once knew of a Robert Browning Society that, in its day, attracted romantic young women but finally dwindled to a few old ladies who couldn't bear not to meet any more. In fact, because one of those last old ladies was a friend, I ended up with the society's archives.

But on the whole, membership helped hold Middle Americans together in common purpose, reinforcing many of the values that have moved us to be contributors to the common good. And what could be wrong with that?

Music

———◆———

THIS IS THE CLARENCE OLSON JUNIOR HIGH SCHOOL BAND OF 1958-'59. I'M ON THE RIGHT END OF THE FRONT ROW WITH MY OBOE. THE BOY WITH THE TUBA IN BACK IS TOM NEVILLE, SUBJECT OF THE EARLIER "COURAGE" CHAPTER. — PHOTO COURTESY OF DEWANE STUDIO, WOODSTOCK, ILLINOIS

"Glad you saw Elvis Presley. I think I would like to see him, although I have never been overly excited about his type of music." — Part of a letter from my mother to my pregnant wife, November 23, 1971, just after we saw an Elvis concert in Kansas City.

It might seem logical to assume that the soundtrack of the lives of Middle Americans, especially those of us who grew up in the 1950s and '60s, was nothing but rock 'n' roll. But it turns out we're a lot less one-dimensional than that in our music as well as in the rest of our lives.

For sure we were there when Bill Haley and the Comets kicked things off with their 1954 recording of the 1952 song "Rock Around the Clock," and we spent hours and hours plugged into our favorite radio disc jockeys offering us the week's Top Forty (why forty?). In the Chicago area in my junior high and high school days that mostly meant Dick Biondi and other jocks on radio station WLS.

We knew the Elvis songs, the stuff by the Platters, Four Seasons, Temptations and on and on into harder rock later. And we knew the slow ballads that drew us close to our partners at the noon dances at Clarence Olson Junior High School and at parties at the homes of friends.

But something else was at work, too. There was lots of music left over from the days of our parents and grandparents, and you could hear that music on lots of radio stations. At 8:15 every morning, for instance, on radio station WIND in Chicago you could hear music by Guy Lombardo. An hour and fifteen minutes later WIND was playing Bing Crosby songs, and an hour after that Kate Smith was singing on that station. Beyond that, it was hard to miss country and/or western music coming at us from radio stations and at county fairs we attended.

There were music teachers at our schools helping us learn the songs and band pieces that we'd play for our parents at occasional concerts and for contests. When my sister Mary was in eighth grade she and seven other girls formed an ensemble that performed "The Bluebird of Happiness," not only in a special school gathering but also at nursing homes and for ladies' clubs. Mary, like me, also took piano lessons from more than one teacher. She remembers that Eleanor Masslich, a wonderful member of our church, tried without much success to turn her and me into pianists. Mary says the only piece she ever learned was "The Minute Waltz." My own version of that song dissolved into chaos long before sixty seconds were up.

Toward the end of seventh grade, when I returned from India, where I learned to play the tablas (drums), I took up the oboe and played it in band and orchestra all the way through high school. If you play the oboe you necessarily have to expand your repertoire beyond rock 'n' roll. And there was sacred and classical music, too, some of which we got in church, some of which we caught on records our parents insisted on playing and some of which we heard on radio and TV stations as we scanned what was available.

I even went to music camp at the University of Wisconsin in Madison one high school summer. There I learned to appreciate classical music more and I even took an introductory course in conducting. I also performed in various musicals in high school, including "The Wizard of Oz" and "Finian's Rainbow." My schoolmates one year also did "Oklahoma!" but without me.

In my own family, most of the musical talent went to my oldest sister, Karin, who wound up as a Juilliard School of Music pipe organ graduate. When Karin was in high school, she and a small group of friends created this or that "combo," as they called it, and practiced in our front room before there was much rock 'n' roll. Even though Karin wound up as the music professional, over the years my three sisters and I played lots of different instruments and performed with lots of musical groups, both instrumental and voice. Today my self-chosen Pandora radio stations on my iPad tend toward classical, such as cellist Yo-Yo Ma, and the great Mozart but also include such artists as Ali Akbar Khan, a master of Indian music; the Beatles; Bob Dylan; the Chanticleer group; classical guitarist Christopher Parkening and Gustav Mahler.

I am glad I still have the photo of me in eighth-grade sitting with dozens of others in our junior high orchestra uniforms. I also was drum major in eighth grand and then part of the color guard in our high school marching band, which performed on the same field on which an annual (and national) drum and bugle corps contest was held. That stirring music thrilled and enthralled me when I was growing up. Beyond that, every Wednesday evening in the summertime a community band (in which I played once or twice) would perform from the bandstand on The Square, and the repertoire ranged from popular tunes to marches to love songs.

The kind of diversity represented by our music was also reflected in Middle Americans' preferences in literature, television shows, theater, sports and other activities. Yes, many of us stuck to reading the best-selling books even if sometimes they were mindless trash. And, yes, many of us watched the spirit-crushing television sit-coms and empty-headed dramas that sold the most soap. But as a minority report you could find Middle Americans tasting Nobel-winning literature from many countries and being regulars at the PBS NewsHour each evening. You'd find we had season tickets to live theater in the cities where we lived and you'd find that our tastes in sports ranged past pro football and baseball to soccer, rugby, lacrosse and women's golf.

So although Middle Americans' preferences in all these things as well as in politics cover a wide range, the common denominator generally has been a willingness to explore new venues ourselves or at least let others have the freedom to do that if we were simply stuck in our ways. That means Middle Americans are weekend campers and people who wouldn't go camping if you paid them $5,000 a day. They are great baseball fans and they are people who ask how many innings it takes to get to half time. They are world travelers and they are people who have never left the Oklahoma panhandle.

What they cherish — what, in fact, some of them have fought and died for — is the freedom to choose whether to watch one of three hundred TV stations tonight or, instead, go to a midweek praise service at church. They want the freedom to vote for this or that politician and the freedom to gripe about him or her in office. They want the freedom to move from Indiana to Montana for a job and the liberty to abandon Montana for Michigan when something better comes along — even though that kind of jumping around is much more likely for younger Middle Americans than it has been for those near or past retirement age.

This lust for liberty was expressed, appropriately enough, in a song written by David Byrne that a lot of us heard as we grew up, "Don't Fence Me In."

Losing

THERE'S NO BETTER PROOF THAT I UNDERSTAND LOSING THAN MY BEING A MEMBER OF THE EMIL VERBAN MEMORIAL SOCIETY, NAMED AFTER THE CHICAGO CUBS' 1948-'50 SECOND BASEMAN. IN 2,911 MAJOR LEAGUE AT BATS HE HIT ONE HOME RUN, CAUSING MY FELLOW VERBAN SOCIETY MEMBER, THE SYNDICATED COLUMNIST GEORGE WILL, TO SAY THAT VERBAN BEST SYMBOLIZED "MEDIOCRITY UNDER PRESSURE."

I didn't grow up as a fan of the Chicago Cubs without learning the benefits of losing. As we Cubs' fans say, anyone can have a bad century.

But even before some of us Middle Americans picked up on the lessons of losing on a professional level, we learned how to lose on our own amateur level — and not expect to get compensated for it with ribbons or trophies just for participating. We played pick-up baseball without adult supervision on school playgrounds after school and on weekends, and we discovered that sometimes you win and sometimes you lose and much of that outcome is determined by innate ability, raw athleticism and effort. In other words, sometimes you deserve to lose because you're no damn good.

It turned out that all of us young athletes were different. For instance, I was a fast runner in grade school. But I didn't like to get hit by kids bigger than me while playing touch football or even get hit by baseballs that took bad hops and slammed into my gut. My buddy Ted Krueger, by contrast, wasn't fast at all, but he was happy to bowl people over, especially later when he was a lineman on our high school football team.

So we drifted toward the activities that most suited our makeup. I moved eventually toward junior high and high school basketball after having been stuck as the second-string third baseman for the Senators in Woodstock's Teen-er League (unless my memory is faulty and this was earlier in the Midget League, as it was called). The first-string third baseman was Lynn — sometimes called Doug — Stewart, who later played as a lineman for a University of Illinois football team that included later Pro Football Hall of Fame member Dick Butkus and that went to the Rose Bowl.

Once late in a game, I overheard Lynn generously suggest to our coach, Dwayne Raney, that he put me in the game. The coach refused, wanting (I much later understood) nothing to do with the idea that every kid should play just because he is on the team. No, the coach wanted the best team out there. That meant I was stuck on the bench — learning how to lose individually even if it meant winning as a team.

Winning is overrated, partly because the stark, no-nuance terms winning and losing so often are attached to relatively trivial pursuits — from baseball games to drag races to the accumulation of obscene amounts of wealth. What have you won when you've won? That's a good question that we Middle Americans have learned to ask. If the answer is "not much," then you have to ask yourself why you're even playing unless it's just for the fun or the exercise — both excellent reasons to play.

What we also have learned about losing is that it's often temporary and leads to something bigger and better than winning might have. Think of Japan. Think of Germany. Would they be the civilized leaders they are today had they won World War II? Not a chance. They came back to good lives for their citizens at least partly because they lost — and had help recovering and adopting values that are laudable, not menacing and brutal.

So we Middle Americans have come not to fear losing, not to imagine that it would be somehow both final and fatal. The damn Cubs fill Wrigley Field with fans almost every game and make good money not because they are fabulous winners, after all.

I'm not suggesting that we love losing and look forward to each opportunity to do it more decisively. No, no. But winning-losing postulates a binary, black-white, up-down world when, in fact, the world is much more complex than that. So we try to take the long view, which hopes and works for success but realizes that what may be seen as a win today will tomorrow be counted as loss — and vice versa. That's useful wisdom for a whole nation.

For me personally the counter-cultural Beatitudes in the fifth chapter of the Gospel of Matthew are instructive in this. Jesus turned his world upside down in that sermon, saying the one who mourns is blessed, not the one who is garlanded with the wreathe of victory. In the same way, the story of Jesus' Passion reveals final victory being possible by going through loss — in this case crucifixion. Indeed, one of the things that attracts me to Christianity is that God comes to us in weakness, not strength. God comes to us as a baby. God comes to us as a nailed-to-the-cross loser criminal. And God doesn't celebrate or cause all this evil. Rather, God promises one day to set it all to rights.

Losing: It gets a bad press. We Middle Americans understand why sometimes it's exactly what we need, and we're not afraid to open our arms to it and feel its transformative embrace. See? Or did I lose you?

Sports

ERNIE BANKS — DEPICTED HERE AS A KANSAS CITY MONARCH BY MY SON-IN-LAW, HALLMARK MASTER
ARTIST STEVE WILLAREDT — WAS MY CHILDHOOD SPORTS HERO. — Artwork courtesy of Steve Willaredt.

The makeshift pitching mound in our front yard at 415 West South Street was right next to our tallest tree. So if you spanked a line-drive slightly to the right of directly up the middle there was a chance the ball would bang off the trunk of the tree and lurch right back at you.

Lots of sports for kids in the 1950s were similarly ad hoc. We made up our own fields of dreams. We made up the rules of the game — sometimes in the middle of a play. We gathered together our own teams from neighborhood strays and other incompetent but enthusiastic players. What all this impermanence did, in the end, was to help make us Middle Americans flexible, creative and resourceful. We'd need those qualities, given the headwinds we'd face as adults.

When I was in grade school, my friends and I would gather at the playground at Dean Street School or on a high school field up the street from my house. Or, less than 150 feet from our yard, we'd collect in a vacant (it no longer is) lot at the northeast corner of Hayward and West South streets (Google Earth it). It was in that lot that I first heard someone say "Fuck!" I almost immediately tried saying it to myself. I liked the feel of it in my mouth, though I had no idea of its meaning. So when the game was over I went back home and used the word in front of my oldest sister, Karin. She came unglued and told me never, ever, ever, ever, ever to say that in front of our parents, especially our mother, even though Karin and I, along with my sisters Barbara and Mary, were persuasive biological evidence that Mom not only knew what the word meant but that she and Dad knew how to perform the action to which it referred.

Over the years I've had numerous occasions to say "Fuck!" while playing sports, mostly under my breath to myself about my performance. I've also been able to give thanks that I learned early in life that sports were to be kept in some kind of reasonable perspective. While on the court or field we learned to try to do our best and to care if we won or lost. (See the previous chapter on losing.) But in the long run other things mattered much more and even if we were running with the ball the wrong way on a football field (Bob Blocksom, my freshman girlfriend's brother, once did that in a high school game) we knew that this was not an error that would end our lives.

Sports — especially the organized variety — also taught us the Benedictine virtue of humility, along with patience. Earlier I told you the story of being the second-string third baseman behind Lynn Stewart, and of his suggesting to our coach, Dwayne Raney, that he let me play third. Dwayne told him no. So I sat on the bench until the game ended. I came to understand that there were some things in life at which I simply sucked, while there were other things at which I excelled. The trick was to figure out which was which and to aim my life toward the latter. I could have whipped Lynn Stewart in a writing or speech-making contest, but he had me dead to rights in any sporting venue (well, maybe not playing "H-O-R-S-E" on the basketball court).

So we Middle Americans learned to pick our battles, stick to our natural skills, be fairly conservative about jumping from job to job, from career to career because, in the end, most of us knew our strengths as well as our weaknesses. And we knew that sometimes it takes us longer than others to develop our strengths.

In high school, for instance, I had a decent — though not a reliable — jump shot. But I continued to work on it even as a college freshman playing intramural basketball. And it finally became something I could depend on — first from twelve to fourteen feet out and finally from seventeen or eighteen feet out and occasionally even farther. One night as a thirty-something adult I played in a pick-up game at a YMCA in the Kansas City area and scored 1.3 million points, nearly all with my seventeen-foot jump shot from left of — and beyond — the foul line. I have no idea why no one seemed to defend against me that evening but I think I didn't miss more than two shots all night. Swish, swish, swish. If I'd had that shot in high school I'd have been a starter instead of a bench warmer for the Woodstock Blue Streaks. And maybe my Blue Streaks might have joined the Green Giants from up the road in Hebron, Illinois, as a state champion from Illinois. The Hebron legacy is one we grew up with and it constantly reminded us that we could succeed against enormous odds.

But even though Hebron was always on our minds, in the end patience, humility, acceptance of one's gifts and an understanding of one's limitations are characteristics of Middle Americans, though they're not universally shared. There are, of course, Middle Americans who think they are poets or song writers or potters or interior designers when, in fact, they are pitiful amateurs producing schlock. But on the whole, we Middle Americans have tended to find our seventeen-foot jump shot lanes and have stayed in them. In my own career, for instance, I spent three-plus years in my first job as a reporter for the now-defunct *Times-Union* newspaper in Rochester, New York, and then moved to my second post at *The Kansas City Star*. Although I reinvented myself several times while at *The Star*, I stayed within my skill zone full time for most of forty years there. And this longevity was not altogether unusual for people of my generation. Now, of course, it is more likely that people will change jobs much more often as well as entire career fields, and although some of that flexibility and risk-taking is to be admired, I wonder whether people who make so many changes have lost a sense of their own abilities and limitations.

Perhaps the most important thing sports taught me and other Middle Americans was, as I wrote in the previous chapter, how to lose — and get over it. Our Woodstock teams did a lot of losing, though there was the occasional conference championship to celebrate. Beyond that, those of us who grew up as fans of the Chicago Cubs, even those of us whose childhood heroes included the fabulous Ernie Banks of the Cubs, had no choice but to learn about losing. As I write this, the Cubs have just played in their one hundred and fifth season of rebuilding since their last World Series win in 1908, the year before my father was born. And the last time the Cubs were even in the World Series was the year I was born, 1945, when all but the lame and invalid were still in military uniforms.

Losing is not something we learned to love, just something we knew was an inevitable part of living. That does not mean that we accepted unacceptable losses, such as tens of thousands of our soldiers killed in morally indefensible wars in Vietnam and Iraq, say. Or that we didn't care that the public lost faith in government because of Vietnam, Watergate, Iran Contra, Monica Lewinsky, Iraq and many other scandals and terrible decisions. Those things we found disgusting. Those things we sometimes took to the streets to resist and protest.

But you can't take to the streets over every small matter. You have to know when to go, when to stay and when to ignore it all. That's what sports helped to teach me and many other Middle Americans. That and the reality that we don't all deserve medals and ribbons just for showing up.

Yes, sports taught us the conventional wisdom of teamwork, of practice, practice, practice, of being competitive without being compassionless. But it also taught us the unalloyed joy of a moment of success. I remember the thrill as a 10-year-old of racing from one side of the Dean Street playground to the other one recess and beating every kid in the race. It was an orgasmic high, though I couldn't have described it that way then.

Later, in my thirties, I was playing the fourth outfield position, called a short fielder, on a *Kansas City Star* softball team one evening. We were ahead by a run in the bottom of the last inning. The other team had the tying run at third base and one out when the batter sent a sharp line drive off to my right. I ran hard and snared the ball in the web of my glove, whirled and threw to third to double off that runner and win the game. Of course in the ultimate pattern of the cosmos it meant nothing. But there was an ecstasy to it that is hard to describe — different from the ecstasy of seeing my children born and not nearly as important, but an ecstasy nonetheless.

And we Middle Americans can tell the difference between such ecstasies, meaning that, in the end, we generally don't confuse our priorities terribly. When people riot after a World Series or Super Bowl victory, we're the ones standing off to the side (meaning not present at the rumble) wondering what the hell is wrong with these people.

It's often a good question to ask, and we Middle Americans are not reluctant to ask it, thanks to what sports has helped to teach us.

Race

THIS IS WHAT FOUR WHITE, EURO-CENTRIC CHILDREN FROM WOODSTOCK PRODUCED BY MARRYING (OR, MORE
TO THE POINT, MOSTLY OUR CHILDREN MARRYING) PEOPLE OF JAPANESE, KOREAN, FILIPINO, CHINESE AND
AFRICAN-AMERICAN DESCENT.

"You should have heard the violent protest in our (women's church) circle today by some who thought the Presbyterian General Assembly had lost its mind by giving $10,000 to the Angela Davis (defense) Fund. I was telling Daddy about it and he said, 'If I wanted an unbiased opinion on any race question, I certainly know I wouldn't go to anybody over 55 in McHenry County." — From a May 24, 1971, letter from my mother. Davis, a black member of the Communist Party USA, was acquitted of suspected involvement in the August 1970 abduction and murder of a California judge.

"I am 57… When I was 29, I gave birth to a son who is bi-racial. My father would have nothing to do with us for 2 1/2 yrs. I think he was afraid of what others in the town would think. He did finally embrace him and has grown to have a very profound love for him. Let the children lead the way." — Part of a Woodstock native's March 2013 post on the "I Grew up in Woodstock" Facebook page.

"Racism in Woodstock does not seem to be something with much more than a few innocent occurrences such as the Boy Scout minstrel show as a fund raiser with many of the town leaders involved and the carnival (African dip) dunk tank." — Part of a male Woodstock native's April 2012 post on that same Facebook page.

In many ways I was blessed as a child to break out of the essentially all-white cocoon that was Woodstock. When I was in fifth grade, my father accepted an offer to be part of a University of Illinois agriculture team for two years in India and moved our family to that wildly diverse nation of immigrants.

So in that way I'm perhaps not a typical Middle American, but I have watched the slow evolution of thinking about race among other Middle Americans and am both glad for the progress made and astonished at how deep racism's roots run. Racism is a dandelion of persistency and it mostly grows in the soil of ignorance, which produces fear, and in the soil of isolation, which produces both fear and falsehood.

My own nuclear (and later, extended) family is a rather remarkable model of how white Middle Americans (and for sure not all Middle Americans are white or of European origin) have evolved over the decades in their thinking and acting about racial matters. My mother was the daughter of Swedish immigrants. In fact, her first language was Swedish. So near the end of her life when she'd nod off in a comfortable chair on a soft afternoon, she'd sometimes talk in her sleep and speak not English but Swedish. My father was the grandson of German immigrants. But because Dad's father had married the daughter of German immigrants, Dad's heritage was fully German.

So my parents and my three sisters and I were deeply European-American. But my parents used to speak to my three sisters and me about the equality of all human beings before God's eyes and — whether they meant that or not — we ultimately believed them. But that belief took most of a generation to manifest itself in visible ways within our family. It started when Mary, my youngest sister, married a Japanese-American who had been born in one of the World War II prison-isolation camps in Arizona. Their first child, a Japanese-Swedish-German-American daughter, married a Korean-American, who also had Scandinavian blood in him. And in that niece's generation things in our family fairly quickly went international. Another niece married a Filipino-American. Another married a Chinese-American. And yet another married an African-American. At a reunion we look like families of United Nations General Assembly diplomats on a picnic.

I'm confident that if we were to hold a family reunion in Woodstock today we might get a few odd looks but essentially we'd be welcomed and not considered any kind of threat. It was not always so, and my experience of coming to terms with racial equality was, in essence, the experience of much of Middle America. We needed to be freed from our prejudice, our fear, our unthinking willingness to believe traditional wisdom about race, wisdom that was an embarrassment to useful tradition and contained no wisdom at all. It took the Civil Rights Movement, with all that meant, to begin to peel off the misinformation and even hatred that — whether we admitted it or not — had infected our souls. Jimmy Carter spoke for me and for many Middle Americans when he said that Martin Luther King Jr. freed not only blacks but also whites, including him.

When I was a boy in Woodstock there was only one black family (with two or three branches) and only one Jewish family. Oh, we had a few immigrants from such places as Poland but that was the extent of our diversity except for the seasonal influx of Spanish-speaking migrant workers to harvest vegetables and other crops. When we'd drive into Chicago, an hour-plus away, and see African-Americans on the streets, my mother sometimes (especially early in my life) would call them "darkies" or perhaps she merely tolerated us children calling them that. I never heard her or Dad use the toxic term nigger, but I certainly heard it from others, though talk of race and black people was pretty rare.

We were, however, marinated in racist thinking. For instance, when I was in Boy Scouts in the mid-1950s, I rehearsed for a traditional minstrel show that required the boy actors and singers to put on blackface and tell "Rastus and Remus" jokes to a large audience in the high school auditorium. I have copies of the 1956, 1957 and 1958 programs from those minstrel shows. And although I am included in a group photo on the back of the 1956 program, the event itself took place a couple of months after I already had moved to India with my family. So even though I remember rehearsing for the show, I was never an on-stage participant in the real event — but of course would have been had we not left the country.

The 1957 show received several promotional news stories in the *Woodstock Daily Sentinel*, which noted that the boys presenting the minstrel show were part of Boy Scout Troop 124, sponsored by First Presbyterian Church, the congregation to which my family and I belonged (I became a confirmed member in 1958 after returning from India). Indeed, in the 1956 minstrel program the church's pastor, Cecil C. Urch, is listed as "Institutional Representative," while in the programs from the 1957 and 1958 shows he is listed simply as one of the "producers & directors" or a member of the "Committee Men."

My point in noting all this church connection is so that it's clear that a Mainline Protestant church in the 1950s in northern Illinois saw nothing wrong with sponsoring a show of songs and jokes in which adolescent boys wore blackface and pretended to be African-Americans. This was the racial atmosphere Woodstock and much of Middle America was breathing then. And for context, let's remember that the Montgomery Bus Boycott, which began with Rosa Parks refusing to take a seat in the back of a bus in Alabama, started on December 1, 1955. The news about black people refusing to take it anymore apparently was slow getting from Montgomery to Woodstock.

Thanks to my childhood friend Bob Okeson, who performed in these minstrel shows, I have in my possession not just the programs but also a copy of the song lyrics sung in the 1957 performance — called, none-too-subtly, "Plantation Days." The opening number was "There's Nothing Like a Minstrel Show." Other songs included "Ole Dan Tucker," which began, "I come to town de udder night, I hear de noise an' see de fight…" The script obviously tried to help the white boys figure out allegedly black dialect. Finally, after renditions of "Short'nin' Bread" and "Old Black Joe," the show ended with "Lazy Bones," which began this way: "Lazy-bones, Sleepin' in the sun, How you 'spec' to get your day's work done…"

How, indeed? The obvious message was that these lazy-boned black people needed someone like a Simon Legree from *Uncle Tom's Cabin* to whip (literally) them into shape. It was a message that sank deep into the marrow of many white Middle Americans.

All of this might have been more understandable had it taken place a hundred years earlier in the Chicago area. In fact, something quite like it did. As historian Richard Lawrence Miller reports in Volume Three of his excellent four-volume biography *Lincoln and His World*, Abraham Lincoln himself, who later would be credited with freeing America's slaves, attended and enjoyed minstrel shows. Miller reports that one of Lincoln's friends, Henry Whitney, recalled this about a Chicago performance of one:

"On or about the 23d day of March, 1860, only a few weeks before the sitting of the Chicago (Republican presidential nomination) convention, he (Lincoln) was attending the United States Court, being then quite a candidate for the Presidency. I had three tickets presented to me for Ramsey & Newcomb's Minstrels, a high-toned troupe, and I asked him if he would like to go to a 'nigger show' that night; he assented rapturously; his words were: 'Of all things I would rather do tonight, that suits me exactly,' and I never saw him apparently enjoy himself more than he did at that entertainment. He applauded as often as anybody, and with greater heartiness. The nondescript song and dance of Dixie was sung and acted by this troupe, the first time I ever saw it, and probably the first time it was sung and acted in Illinois. I can remember well the spontaneity of Lincoln's enthusiasm, and the heartiness of his applause at the music and action of this rollicking and eccentric performance. ... He clapped his great brawny hands in true rustic heartiness and exclaimed, in riotous enthusiasm: 'Let's have it again! Let's have it again.'"[23]

And yet in that same era — more than a hundred years before the Woodstock Boy Scouts offered a minstrel show to parents, grandparents and friends — there was at least some public sentiment suggesting that such blackface entertainment was not just racist but profoundly immoral. On the same page on which Miller quotes Henry Whitney's minstrel show recollection, he also quotes this editorial about minstrel shows from what is called "A Massachusetts Paper" that was reprinted in the *Sangamo Journal*, a Springfield, Illinois, newspaper, on August 7, 1845:

"The performers of these 'melodies' doubtless consider themselves superior to the colored race; and proud of their white skins, look down upon a negro with contempt. Yet they go to the Southern plantations, and catch the words of the unconnected songs of slaves degraded by a long period (of) servitude, and debarred from the slightest intellectual culture, added to these words the most ineffably nonsensical productions of their own stupid brains, then endeavor to make their countenance resemble, as nearly as possible, those of the negroes whom they affect to despise — take the instruments which these wretched beings use, or devise others of so harsh a sound that no savage would endure them, and appear before the public, offering them what they style a 'grand, original, chaste, and delightful entertainment.' Perhaps the thought never occurred to them they are, in reality, voluntarily sinking themselves to a far lower state of debasement than that in which the negroes are unfortunately placed.

"'Entertainments' of this kind are outrages upon all good taste and refinement, if they are not decidedly immoral in their tendency; and it is to be hoped, that they will be speedily supplanted by amusements of a moral, rational, and elevated character."[24]

But more than a century later in Woodstock it was as if no one ever had raised an objection to minstrel shows. It was as if the Civil War had never been fought, the Emancipation Proclamation never issued, the first stirrings of the Civil Rights Movement had yet to happen. And all these years later the memories of having even rehearsed for a minstrel show embarrass me and break my heart.

Not long ago the memory of these mid-1950s minstrel shows surfaced in comments on the "I Grew Up in Woodstock" Facebook page, and I was quite taken by the oft-expressed idea that racism was rampant in Woodstock then, coupled with a few comments that tried to soften that clear reality. The few people seeking to explain (not excuse; they know and acknowledge that minstrel shows are seen now as inherently racist) what happened in the 1950s insisted that all this minstrel show stuff was done in good fun and that no one — black or white — should have or would have taken offense back then. In other words, there was precious little idea at the time that "Amos and Andy" or "Stepin Fetchit" were anything but sources of innocent humor. It didn't mean to be racist, was the argument, and thus it wasn't.

But, of course, white Middle Americans never experienced this kind of derisive humor from the perspective of the people of color who were the butt of the jokes. So white Middle Americans simply have no standing to dismiss criticism that labels minstrel shows of the 1950s and before as inherently racist.

It's not so surprising that an essentially all-white small town could put on a minstrel show in the mid-1950s and imagine that it was simply entertainment. Residents of Woodstock at the time — and, indeed, many Middle Americans then — were simply enmeshed in a culture in which bigotry was so common that it seemed normal and acceptable. For instance, on page 11 of the June 6, 1957, *Woodstock Daily Sentinel* you can find this headline: "File Suit to Stop Japs from Trying William Gerard." Twelve years after the end of World War II, our local newspaper was still using the derogatory term Japs. And if you look in the classified ads of the *Sentinel* in that era you find help wanted ads divided into "Male" and "Female," reflecting the common practice then that reserved certain jobs just for men and others just for women. Beyond that, if you look at the 1959-'60 list I have of "band mothers" from Woodstock Community High School you will discover that each woman is a "Mrs." (no single mothers, apparently) and all but five of the eighty-three women are identified not by their own first name but by their husband's first name. This kind of prejudice and cultural myopia was pervasive, and it mostly seemed like the expected ordering of the universe to most Middle Americans then.

The reality was that most of us Middle Americans grew up benefiting hugely from what sociologists now call "white privilege," but we were so deeply entangled in it that only when those outside our system began to point it out and question it did we even recognize the sea in which we swam. Eventually, however, many Middle Americans did come to understand that they were part of a system that routinely gave advantages to one on the basis of race just as it denied rights, privileges and advantages to another on that same basis. Even today not all Middle Americans recognize that reality but many more do so than when I was a child. And today the issues of diversity go far beyond black and white. They also go to the many immigrants who have come to our shores since the 1965 immigration reform act was signed into law by President Lyndon B. Johnson and they especially go to the many religions those immigrants brought with them.

When I write or give speeches about interfaith dialogue these days, I often say that if the call of the Twentieth Century to Americans was to get racial harmony right (an unfinished task), the call of the Twenty-first Century is to get religious harmony right. And that, clearly, is also unfinished business as we wrestle with what it means to have Hindu and Buddhist temples, Islamic mosques and Sikh gurdwaras in neighborhoods that traditionally have been home only to Christian churches or Jewish synagogues.

As I say, this coming to terms with racial and ethnic differences was a slow process. When I went off to college at the University of Missouri in Columbia in 1963 I had no idea who my roommate might be in the dorm to which I was assigned. I remember Mom asking me if I would be bothered if he turned out to be a black kid. Of course not, I said, though I will now confess that I secretly hoped to ease into better race relations more slowly with, perhaps, a black kid or two down the hall, though not in my own room. As it turned out, I wound up rooming with a white Missouri farm boy for four years — two in the dorm, two in apartments — and the dorm black kids were confined (by choice or chance, I didn't know) to rooms on the dorm's bottom floor, called The Grotto. Choice? Maybe, but I doubt it.

In Woodstock, Illinois, in the 1950s — and in much of Middle America — most of those of us who were white simply assumed that we were the human norm, we were in charge, we were the way God intended people to be. Insulation and isolation tend to produce such malformed assumptions, and I'm pretty sure that people in remote villages in southern India or western China felt the same way then about themselves. It takes exposure to the wider world to help us understand where we fit in the breathtakingly broad human picture. It took us Middle Americans too long to recognize how pinched was the view of humanity that our cultural isolation and insulation had given us, but eventually, as I say, many of us began to see ourselves as part of a much broader context. And it helped that our children began to fall in love with people who came from ethnicities and cultures different from ours.

When we finally began to open up to this reality, the Human Genome Project came along and told us that biologically there is no such thing as race anyway. What we call race is primarily a political or cultural construct. That's information most of us still are processing, uncertain whether it can possibly be right. But what we do know is that the white cocoon that was Woodstock in the 1950s has burst forth in a rather remarkable rainbow. And for that I'm grateful.

I saw clear evidence of this rainbow when I attended a football game in September 2013 between my alma mater and the team from the new high school in town, Woodstock North. In the stands cheering the teams on were blacks, whites, Hispanics and Asians. And they reflected the makeup of the students enrolled at the schools today, though that student population continues to be overwhelmingly white. But neither the Woodstock High junior varsity nor the varsity football teams I watched play was all white.

One of my classmates from the graduating class of 1963, also at the game as part of our fiftieth high school reunion, turned to me and pointed to the black kid on the sidelines wearing number 34.

"That's my grandson," he said, his voice full of pride. "My daughter has two adopted black children."

When we were graduating, no one in Woodstock could have or would have uttered such a sentence. But today Middle Americans not only have witnessed this kind of change but at times have either led it or simply let it happen because their only other choice was to move to the radical fringe of a changing society. And that's not where Middle Americans live.

Politics

I WAS MOWING THIS YARD AND ANOTHER ONE AROUND THE CORNER THE DAY I SURPRISED MYSELF BY SINGING A JFK CAMPAIGN SONG ALOUD IN 1960.

"Nixon is the most insensitive man in the world, especially in the race area....We simply cannot afford Richard Nixon. And if you vote for him, you're no friend of mine. Worse, you're no friend to yourself." — A subtle letter from me to my parents, April 24, 1968.

"There is enough (Watergate) evidence on the record now to indicate a serious attempt by people in very high office to sabotage the vital political processes of our country, and I do not understand how we can afford to endorse that kind of illegal, immoral activity by voting for the man (Richard Nixon) who must, because of his position, accept ultimate responsibility. And have you asked yourselves what will happen if the subsequent trials in all of this reveal a direct link to 1600 Pennsylvania Avenue? We will have a Constitutional crisis on our hands..." — From a prophetic October 21, 1972, letter from me to my parents.

I often tell people that I didn't meet a Democrat in Woodstock or McHenry County until I was in eighth grade. It's a bit of a stretch but not much.

My recollection is that when I was in junior high or early high school the first Democrat to be elected countywide since the Civil War took office — the sheriff. Clearly our town and the whole county were landslides for the Republican Party.

But this was not the GOP of the modern Tea Party or similar aberrations that embrace uncompromising rigidity as a foundational political principle. This was the GOP of Ike, of Abe Lincoln and other Republicans who were sensible, patriotic, wise people. My former and late father-in-law, who was from Upstate New York, was like that. Dick Bloom once served as GOP chairman of Orleans County, and though we had our political differences, he was the sort of Republican who gave the party a good name.

I remember the first time I learned that within the high political walls of Woodstock there were a few Democrats. The day after the 1952 presidential election I was walking into Dean Street School to go to my second grade class when I ran into Melodee Church, who told me her father was practically in tears that morning because Adlai Stevenson had lost the election. I could not make this information compute. Who would have been in favor of the Democrat? Everybody else I knew was happy that Dwight D. Eisenhower had been elected. Adlai Stevenson? Seriously?

Then when I was in high school I came to the realization that within my own spirit there could be found certain tentative Democratic leanings. One day in the middle of the 1960 presidential race between Richard M. Nixon and John F. Kennedy I was mowing the Hanrahan family's lawn across the street from our house and their rental property around the corner when I realized I was singing aloud (though I doubted that it could be heard over the roar of the mower) one of the JFK campaign songs: "I'm going down to Washington to shake hands with President Kennedy. . ."

After the words slipped out, I looked around to see if anyone had noticed. No. I was alone. But I told myself I'd better be careful with such heretical thinking.

Eventually, because of good history teachers at the University of Missouri, I accommodated myself to the reality that not only were there lots of Democrats in the world but that some of them, such as Harry S. Truman, turned out to be fabulous presidents and some of them, especially before the Civil War, turned out to be disasters. I kept looking for Republicans I thought were in the Abe Lincoln tradition, but they mostly seem to have disappeared, especially after Nixon's mostly disastrous White House time when Ronald Reagan began to shift the party toward the narrow views it often espouses today.

The GOP has moved substantially to the right in recent decades, and although here and there you still can find some wise, honest GOP officeholders, they are growing rare among the icy ideologues.

What I sometimes wonder about these days is how, given our GOP roots, my three sisters and I wound up as people who pretty consistently vote for the Democratic candidate for president and who, though we are not happy being labeled this or that, are not knee-jerk offended when someone calls us progressive or liberal. But whenever anyone slaps that label on me, I insist on the opportunity to unpack what I think it means for me, because it doesn't mean what Rush Limbaugh or Fox "News" commentators say it means.

It may well be that Middle Americans should shoulder a substantial part of the blame for the way our nation's politics have become so divisive. How could it be otherwise, given how many of us there are and how long we've been around?

But I suspect that our failure was one of omission, not so much commission, by which I mean that we often were either apathetic or distracted. We let others take the reins of politics while we worried about other matters, assuming that if we simply showed up on Election Day things would work out all right. Other citizens died so that we could vote, but even our turnout on Election Day has become scandalously low.

It was foolish to think our only responsibility was voting when it was convenient. We allowed ideologues to move into positions of power, people certain of everything, people who were guided by a terribly limited vision of the world and who often were insistent that this vision was somehow divinely approved or sponsored.

And these were ideologues of both the left and the right. Most of the ones on the left got marginalized by the normal processes of debate and position development within the Democratic Party while many of the ones on the right came to power in a Republican Party that had lost its vision, its center, its soul. That's too simple a description but there's plenty of truth in it.

This divisive political atmosphere has managed to attract some of our children to political positions that are either bone-headed or the result of not enough information. But I'm glad that at least they seem less disinterested in the world of politics than many Middle Americans of my generation were.

Perhaps the wounds we Middle Americans suffered at the hands of politicians responsible for Vietnam, for Watergate and for similar scandals and terrible decisions led some of us to give up too easily and to wish a pox on all politicians. We should have recognized that if our government was failing us it was our responsibility to fix it because it is *our* government. Instead, many of us simply complained and walked away.

It's too simplistic to label people as members of the left or the right, as liberals or conservatives. That's the divisive language that people like Limbaugh use to make political points with followers. Still, there is a long continuum of political thinking that stretches from monarchy to anarchy (with some malarkey thrown in). If you want to find Middle Americans along that spectrum, it's best to look in the broad middle. Some will be Republicans, some Democrats, some independents. But almost none will be radicals of any stripe. Rather, they understand that what makes politics works is pragmatism and principled compromise.

Political moderates often tend to be theological moderates, too, which is to say they are not the people who will decisively declare you're doomed to hell because of your heretical beliefs nor are they the people who will say all religions are the same and it doesn't matter what you believe as long as you believe something.

This middleness, so to speak, grows out of a worldview that takes the long view of things and that recognizes how often people in the past have been wrong about strongly held positions. If, by contrast, you are among those who think that "principled compromise" is an oxymoron, you may have no idea what I'm talking about. How sad, both for you and for our divided country.

Business and Money

FOR YEARS AND YEARS, RAY WOLF RAN A JEWELRY STORE JUST OFF THE SQUARE IN WOODSTOCK, OFFERING QUALITY PRODUCTS AND SERVICE. THE STORE IS GONE BUT THE OLD SIGN HANGS ON.

"By now I hope you have all received your surprise Christmas present from the (Helander grandparents) estate. Since there wasn't enough cash on hand to give Ruth and me what was specified in the will, Al Powers (lawyer) suggested we advance the money for you kids and consider the house and farm our legacy…I felt there probably was no better time to send it to you than right now. I do hope you can use it for something special but at least you have cash for now if you need it desperately, without borrowing." — December 10, 1970, letter from my mother to my sisters and me about checks for a few thousand dollars (or maybe just $1,000) each from the estate of Mom's parents.

"…we became too used to two checks and one somehow isn't enough. Oh, it's enough, to be sure, but we seem to live from pay day to pay day as never before." — October 14, 1970, letter from my wife to my parents soon our move from Rochester, New York, to Kansas City, Missouri.

"Bill got a nice raise this week — $100 more per month." — December 1973 letter from my wife to my parents.

Like many Middle Americans, my first personal exposure to business and money had to do with running a neighborhood lemonade stand. Well, for me it also had to do with helping my family sell pop out of a big tank in our driveway when it was Soap Box Derby day because the races started almost in front of our driveway. But even earlier than that, I set up a lemonade stand on the sidewalk in front of our West South Street house and mostly waited. I failed to get rich there, though I did learn a little about grace.

One day some high school kids drove up in a car. One of those big boys got out, came up to me and handed me a dollar. But he didn't want any lemonade. He just gave me a buck and left. I was both mystified and gratified. Almost fifty years later I was visiting Woodstock and discovered that some kids one house down from my old house were selling lemonade from a sidewalk stand. I stopped and told them the story about my free dollar. Then I handed them four quarters and left without getting lemonade. Maybe they learned a bit about grace that day, too, because it's for sure that as I kid I discovered that even a profit-oriented business could produce moments of grace.

Mostly, though, I learned about business and money by watching adults around me. Ray Wolf opened his jewelry store every business day and gave customers fabulous service on watches and other things they'd bought from him sometimes years before. And my classmate Barry Frame operated a men's clothing store on The Square for years. He just showed up each day and tried to offer the public what it wanted, what it needed and better quality than it expected.

THIS OLD HOUSE ON WEST JUDD STREET (WHICH NOW BUMPS UP AGAINST A BRICK OFFICE BUILDING IN A SADLY UNATTRACTIVE WAY) HOUSED MY FATHER'S OFFICE WHEN HE WAS McHENRY COUNTY FARM ADVISER IN THE 1950s.

I saw my father go to the Farm Bureau office each day, where his farm adviser office was located. He never got rich there but he was consistent, friendly, knowledgeable and entrepreneurial. (In fact, my family was never rich when I grew up, though we always were fed, sheltered and clothed and did not think of ourselves as poor.) Ernie Hahn and Stub Collins were at their gasoline service stations each day, models of reliability. And Bob Vieregg was at his "Corner Cupboard" restaurant, always a good place for pie and hot beef sandwiches. And Ernie Bohn was at his hardware store. And around the corner from there was Les Kidoo, a barber. There was also my mother, who represented many of these people in her job as Welcome Wagon hostess.

Everywhere I turned, it seemed, I was seeing people in businesses that made them at least enough money for basics. But more to the point, they were businesses that provided what other people needed to live. The Busse family had flowers for funerals. The Woodstock Dry Goods store, where Arthur (Mac) McCullough ran things, provided bolts of cloth for dresses that needed to be sewn for proms and parties. John Laing ran a hardware store, too.

On a 2012 visit to Woodstock, I ran into my old bakery boss, Carl Jessen, who was visiting his wife's grave at Oakland Cemetery. The summer I graduated from high school Carl paid me $5 each Saturday to help clean his bakery — well, $5, minus 18 cents withheld for Social Security, plus milk and doughnuts.

Carl Jessen created and baked the pastries at the Early American Bakery and Lee Dittman came around to houses and fixed whatever plumbing had gone bust. He'd just walk in the unlocked doors, holler "Plumber!" and go to work.

In addition to all these individual business people there were lots of folks who went to work for big Woodstock employers, such as the Autolite plant, Guardian Electric, various tool and die makers and eventually Morton Salt. Sometimes the folks who were in business for themselves would speak quietly and with some condescension about the poor factory workers whose lives were imagined to be full of drudgery, though, oddly enough, at the same time they spoke with admiration about the farmers at work at the edge of town even though that work was equally repetitive and hard. My own parents from time to time would, well, not exactly threaten but strongly encourage us to do well in school so that we wouldn't end up as factory workers. And because they both had grown up as farm kids, I think they never imagined that we would return to the land as farmers. And we didn't. Neither my three sisters nor I could have been counted among the One Percent of wealthy people in the country against whom the Occupy Wall Street protesters complained, though we got along well enough through our own labor and were helped some in retirement with funds from the estate of my mother's sister, Ruth, who did well investing in the stock market and who had no children of her own.

By trial and error — and not much by formal education, at least through high school — we learned about economic and personal finance. In the summer in which I was graduated from high school I had a Saturday morning job with a friend cleaning Carl Jessen's bakery. I once worked for another man named Carl who ran a nursery at the edge of town that mostly sold plants to Chicago florists and other retailers. This Carl would pay us ninety cents an hour but wouldn't give us any money until we asked for it. Some employees my age tried to leave all their earnings with Carl so they wouldn't blow it on useless stuff. Only later did we figure out that we could have come out ahead had we taken the pay regularly and put it in an interest-bearing account at the bank — say, the ones that Harold Beth or Don Still ran on The Square.

Many of us grew up not knowing much about mortgages, about checking accounts, about interest on credit cards. We had to find out most of that on our own. That ignorance hurt us financially, but the ignorance that was more widespread and more devastating than that had to do with our failure to understand the systemic economic forces that began to pressure and eventually to crush America's middle class, to which most of us belonged. It took us time to recognize how an eighteen percent interest rate and high inflation under Jimmy Carter meant that even with annual salary raises we were losing ground. And it took a while to determine that Ronald Reagan's trickle-down economics was a way of rewarding the people who didn't need to be rewarded and that the reward came at the expense of people who could not afford to be so generous to millionaires. The Middle Americans who never grasped this continued to vote against their own economic self-interest.[25]

Upward mobility was honored as a concept but as a reality it began to lose its luster and its credibility for many Middle Americans. We admired the true entrepreneurs — the Henry Fords, and Thomas Edisons, then later the Bill Gates, the Steve Jobs, the Mark Zuckerbergs and others — and we wished them well and sometimes tried to be among them with our ideas for products and services. But in the end we began to resent the rules of the economic games that kept so many people struggling financially, that kept so many people plugging along at minimum wage and that kept driving jobs overseas.

I know friends today who failed to understand what it would take to retire comfortably and who live on nothing but a Social Security check, having spent the money they might have saved earlier in their lives — sometimes just on necessities to survive. In fact, the Social Security Administration reports that among elderly Social Security beneficiaries, twenty-three percent of married couples and about forty-six percent of unmarried persons rely on Social Security for ninety percent or more of their income.[26] I also know people whose savings and net worth took big hits when the economy tanked in 2008, largely as a result of a wildly run-amok financial system that depended on greed and an almost criminal lack of regulation.

Were Middle Americans responsible for some of this? Of course. But mostly they were slammed by an economic and political system rigged by the people they elected to reward those who already had money and power —money and power used to determine the results of elections. Our lemonade stand histories, our tradition of honoring individual business operators who, we thought, competed on a level playing field — all that romantic, small-town vision of how the economy worked was inadequate to protect us from the global economy of which our country inevitably became a part.

We mostly get it now, but catching up with our failure to imagine the system that eventually got constructed and began operating will take more time than we have. We will have to depend on our children and grandchildren to pick up the pieces. The only trouble is that we have failed to give our children and grandchildren an adequate economic education, and many of them will become victims, too — without a lot of hope for grace.

Institutional Failure

◀━━━━▶

THIS WAS THE CUBICLE IN WHICH I FINISHED MY FULL-TIME CAREER AT *THE KANSAS CITY STAR*. AFTER I RETIRED IN MID-2006, AN ECONOMIC DOWNTURN AND OTHER FACTORS LED TO MANY *STAR* EMPLOYEES LOSING THEIR JOBS. IN LATE 2008, MY WEEKLY FREELANCE FAITH SECTION COLUMN WAS CANCELED FOR ECONOMIC REASONS IN A NEWSPAPER INDUSTRY STRUGGLING TO STAY ALIVE.

"We're in the midst of shock over (Vice President Spiro T.) Agnew's resignation this afternoon. What can possibly be next..." — October 10, 1973, letter from my wife to my parents.

Not long after my high school class graduated in June 1963, the world as we knew it began to unravel in frightening ways. Later in college, when I read William Butler Yeats' classic poem, "The Second Coming,"[27] I had words I could use to describe some of what we were experiencing:

> *Things fall apart; the centre cannot hold;*
> *Mere anarchy is loosed upon the world...*

Oh, there always had been surprises, always corruption, theft, dishonesty, always the shaken memories of our parents and grandparents who had lived through the Great Depression and somehow had learned to trust again. (Surely World War II helped to restore their trust in each other and in social institutions.) And that very trust gave us confidence, gave us reason not to go running toward rebellion, bereft of hope.

But when President John F. Kennedy was murdered on the cruel streets of Dallas, then a city that welcomed radical haters, and when it became obvious to almost everyone but the Warren Commission that something was involved besides the addled brain of Lee Harvey Oswald, we began to look at each other with disbelief and wonder whether now it was our generation's turn to experience institutional failure. It's not that we didn't think Oswald shot Kennedy. The evidence is pretty indisputable that he did. But what drove him to it? Who pulled his puppet strings? How could he have so many ties with the CIA, the Soviet Union, Cuba and the FBI and all of them be meaningless? Clearly our fears about all of this were justified. And even as countless Americans who had been treated as second-class citizens and worse were about to gain some measure of freedom, all Americans were about to lose a secure sense that our public systems and institutions worked reliably, fairly, thoroughly, honestly.

Soon after release of the botched Warren Commission report we began to sink into the bog of Vietnam, with its made-up body counts, its wild miscalculations by minds we were told were the best and the brightest.[28] And from there it was on to Watergate, Iran-Contra, hyper-inflation, a president's astonishing argument about the meaning of "is," another president's declaration of "mission accomplished" in a needless war in which the U.S. wasn't close to accomplishing any worthy mission. And from there it was Katy bar the door. The earlier well-intentioned War on Poverty did not succeed in eliminating its target. The Great Society programs moved some people out of misery but at a high cost that created a bloated poverty-management class. And the middle class that had been brought back to life by FDR's New Deal and Harry Truman's Fair Deal began to find itself squeezed and battered by dying labor unions, outsourced work and a rueful politics that worked well for the rich but hardly anyone else.

Some Middle Americans saw their jobs go first to southern states with lower-cost labor and eventually to manufacturers overseas. The textile and auto industries were among the hardest hit, and Woodstock itself first experienced the closing of its typewriter manufacturing facilities and eventually its huge Autolite plant. In 1935, Electric Autolite acquired the Alemite Die Casting Company in Woodstock to make not just component parts for the company's electric lighting system for cars but also such items as radiator grills, door handles and other automotive hardware. But by the 1970s the factory was gone and the site became not just a largely unregulated landfill but a toxic dump that the Environmental Protection Agency had to help clean up.

In more recent years, of course, Middle Americans saw under-regulated financial institutions run amok on both Wall Street and Main Street. Those failures were catastrophic for many who saw their retirement savings slammed, the value of their homes sink and their jobs disappear. And although it was tempting to blame one or two people — George W. Bush, say, or the head of Fannie Mae — institutional failures inevitably require many villains and many bystanders, some innocent, some not. No doubt among the cast of thousands were some Middle Americans who let loose of their core values and either jumped into (or milked) the sub-prime housing market debt crisis in one way or another or who, against their own self-interest, elected some of the people who either let this debacle happen on their watch or who were directly responsible for the policies that wound up freezing the credit markets, nose-diving the stock market and throwing all kinds of people out of work.

The list of institutions that have failed or badly underserved Middle Americans (sometimes with their help) is long, indeed. It includes American schools that produced students who, in recent tests to see how they stack up against pupils from other developed countries, ranked 25th in math, 17th in science and 14th in reading, according to a Harvard University study.[29] And it includes a criminal justice system that has the highest documented incarceration rate in the world and that has held on to a capital punishment system that almost every other developed nation has abandoned for both financial and moral reasons. While we're counting institutional failures, let's not forget our health insurance system, a baffling collection of rules and procedures that Obamacare is seeking to mitigate for at least some Americans. But nasty partisanship and an incompetent website launch of Healthcare.gov have meant little relief from what is the costliest health care system in the world by almost any measure.

There is, of course, much to love about America and most Middle Americans, including me, wouldn't become ex-patriots for anything. But we are bone-tired of seeing one institution after another sputter and fail to meet the purpose for which it was established. And in many ways we are embarrassed to be handing on to our children and grandchildren a skeleton newspaper business, a gasping-for-air postal service, an unreliable pension/retirement system, a greed-fed Wall Street culture, Mainline churches in precipitous decline and a food safety system that sometimes allows tainted products to reach the shelves of our grocery stores.

At times we Middle Americans feel overwhelmed by the very systems we and our ancestors helped to create. Our angst hasn't yet reached revolutionary heights but we know that we should have done better at managing all of this. We are adaptive people and we have proven that over and over but sometimes it feels as if the waves of change are too high and one day we may sink beneath them for good. Our worries no longer are for us but for our children and grandchildren, to whom we owe some apologies.

Vietnam

My high school classmates Donald Dermont, left, and Sidney Elyea, died in Vietnam in 1966, and still today I am not sure why their deaths were necessary. — Photos from 1963 *Woodcohi* yearbook.

No doubt the great American divide that we now find in our pungent politics and in our churlish, fatuous culture wars can trace some of its causes to the Vietnam War, which wounded our nation's soul, perhaps irreparably.

Some of us Middle Americans fought in that war. Some of us fought against it. Some did both. Like many of my contemporaries, I favored it at first, believing that the Domino Theory held water — the theory that if we let the communists have this or that land eventually they'd take over the world. How foolish of us. The North Vietnamese were not fighting to spread communism around the world. They were fighting a civil war for control of their homeland. Indeed, ultimately communism could not even defend communism, which has fallen moribund because it almost always and almost everywhere betrayed its own best ideals (which were none too good to begin with) — and perhaps had no choice but to do so, given the rapacious greed embedded in the bone and marrow of human nature.

My sophomoric (I was literally a college sophomore then) enthusiasm for the war quickly waned as it became clear that we were killing innocent people in a fight to keep corrupt South Vietnam leaders in power. When I lost my passion for the war, however, I found myself standing against the very war that my contemporaries — some of whom were my friends — were being drafted to fight. Should I have told them not to go? Should I have said they were moral cowards for not resisting? Should I have written to Norma Scott, the head of our Woodstock draft board and a member of the church in which I grew up, to tell her to take me off her mailing list or to drop my draft folder behind a filing cabinet, not to be found until I was way past draft age?

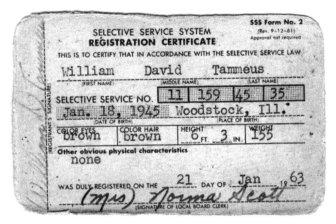

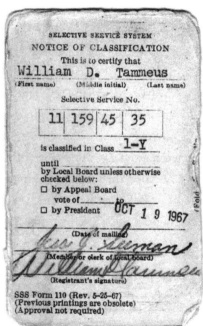

STILL IN MY WALLET TODAY YOU WILL FIND MY DRAFT CARD REGISTRATION AND MY NOTICE THAT I HAVE BEEN CLASSIFIED I-Y, MEANING A TEMPORARY MEDICAL DEFERMENT.

I had been diagnosed with rheumatoid arthritis as a senior in college, so I was ruled medically ineligible for the draft. I was classified 1-Y, a temporary ineligibility, not the more permanent 4-F designation — and I carry my draft card with me even to this day because, well, the card says I must have it with me at all times and we Middle Americans are nothing if not law abiding. So after I was graduated from college, when my four-year student deferment expired, I still was in no danger of being sent to fight. Besides, my weak eyesight made me non-combat qualified. So I had precious little moral ground on which to stand and tell my Woodstock classmates and other contemporaries to do whatever they could to avoid fighting in Vietnam.

As a result — and perhaps for the first time — I understood that sometimes we are part of a system that forecloses the possibility of controlling our own life. I felt like a farmer in the Great Depression who discovers that through no fault of his own his markets have dried up and he no longer can forestall a bank foreclosing on his land. I had read about that in books and heard about that from my parents, though the farms on which they grew up were not lost to foreclosure in that dark time.

But Vietnam was personal. I knew guys who had been drafted to fight in this ugly, loathsome war, guys who had been classmates at Woodstock Community High School. In fact, two of those classmates died in the war, Sidney J. Elyea and Donald Eugene (Geno) Dermont Jr. I have touched their names on the memory wall of the Vietnam Memorial in Washington, D.C. I honor their service, however wrongheaded the leaders were who sent them into death's hungry maw.

Neither Sid nor Geno was a close friend. Indeed, Geno was nearly a year older than me and wound up in our 1963 graduating class only because earlier he had been held back a year. But both were Middle Americans who became fodder for a war gone bad. Under somewhat different circumstances it could have been me having the candle of my life blown out in some disinterested rice paddy or on some inhospitable hill in Southeast Asia.

I think of Geno Dermont every April 11, that being the date of his death in 1966. And I think of Sid Elyea every Groundhog Day, for that was the date of his death in that same bloody year — a year in which I was safely deferred as a student in the University of Missouri School of Journalism. Sid was only about three weeks older than me, having been born the day after Christmas 1944. So both Geno and Sid died in their early twenties. And something in me died then, too — a sense of trust in the wisdom of our leaders. In fact, I think something died in the hearts of almost all Middle Americans because of Vietnam, even in the hearts of people who continued to support the war effort until the last helicopter lifted people from the U.S. Embassy roof in Saigon.

At some fundamental level, we all eventually knew that we had been betrayed by the very people to whom we had given power. It was a discovery we shared with many of our parents, whom we began to suspect didn't know as much as they pretended to. It was a shocking betrayal that we were loathe to admit had skewered us, flayed us open like some lifeless trout ready for the frying pan. We blamed ourselves. How could we have fallen for the rhetoric of patriotism, the high-toned speeches thanking us for standing up for freedom, the false body counts delivered like salvation sermons to sinners convinced of their own guilt? Later, even Defense Secretary Robert McNamara could not believe the lies he told and let stand in the face of countervailing evidence.

What we Middle Americans came away swearing to ourselves was this: You bastards will not fool us like that again. And then we (well, some of us, though not me) elected Richard M. Nixon, whose secret plan for getting us out of Vietnam was, apparently, to desecrate the office of president and let Gerald Ford order the final helicopters to take the final American believers and fighters out of Vietnam. Somebody owes us an apology. Or maybe we voters owe the nation an apology.

As everything was coming untethered in the 1960s, as our friends were dying in a war that was morally unjustifiable, as some among our number were dropping both acid and out, most of us Middle Americans were telling ourselves to hold on, to find our core values, to question authority, yes, but not to assassinate that authority, not to overthrow it violently, not to give into the very kind of mob rule that nearly shook our young nation to its marrow in the 1830s when a young Middle American named Abraham Lincoln was finding his way in Illinois politics and standing against anarchistic gangs who were then threatening the rule of law there and around the country.[30]

And we did hang on. We did search for the values that would sustain us. We did not give into mob psychology, though for sure many of us participated in all kinds of protests against the war.

But if ever we had innocence — a dubious proposition — we lost it in the Vietnam War. We woke up one day aware that our very souls, our very spirits had been raped. Innocence and virginity are fragile conditions, it turns out. We always knew that and mostly we were perfectly willing — despite the preaching we heard against abandoning our virginity — to cave into sexual temptation when the moment was right. But our innocence about governance, about the foundational morality, the intentions of our leaders was something else. Oh, of course we knew that some people in office were venal, autocratic, corrupt. We knew that Will Rogers was, at core, serious about all of that even as he made people laugh about it. What we did not know was that some of those people would jeopardize our very lives for a morally unwarranted cause, for a vision that lacked a foundation built on the inestimable value of human life. That's what took away our breath. That's what covered us with dung. That's what we could not imagine. That's what Vietnam turned in to.

Earth's soil today is full of the ashes and bones of Sid Elyeas, Geno Dermonts and you can fill in the blanks with one or more of the nearly 60,000 names on the Vietnam Memorial wall[31] or the more than 300,000 American wounded (to say nothing of all the Vietnamese who died or were wounded) or those of us who simply had our souls, our spirits pounded into squash by this contemptible war. In some odd and embarrassing ways, I'm glad that Sid and Geno aren't still around to know how despicable was the war that sucked them in, chewed them up and spat out their corpses. And I'm glad we learned a little something from their deaths. We learned that some things are not worth dying for. Some things are stupid and wrong even if a huge majority of our leaders and our citizens — at least at first — think otherwise.

The Vietnam War, in other words, armed Middle Americans with the weapon of discernment and even a little wisdom — painfully gained, to be sure, but gained nonetheless. That, of course, has not prevented our leaders from sending another generation off to die in Afghanistan and Iraq. But it has helped us see that attacking Afghanistan's Taliban leaders for harboring terrorist training camps was justifiable self-defense in the aftermath of the 9/11 terrorist attacks that killed, among others, my own nephew, my sister Barbara's son, while attacking Iraq for having weapons of mass destruction it never had was just ideological excrement. For that discernment, I give thanks to all the Sid Elyeas and Geno Dermonts who perished in Vietnam, graveyard of our national naïveté.

Explaining Evil

THIS IS THE COVER OF THE BOOK I CO-AUTHORED ABOUT THAT PINNACLE OF TWENTIETH CENTURY EVIL, THE HOLOCAUST. WE WROTE IT NOT TO FIND A SILVER LINING IN THE HOLOCAUST. THERE IS NO SUCH THING. BUT WE WANTED TO TELL STORIES OF PEOPLE WHO RISKED THEIR LIVES TO SAVE OTHERS. — REPRINTED FROM *THEY WERE JUST PEOPLE: STORIES OF RESCUE IN POLAND DURING THE HOLOCAUST*, BY BILL TAMMEUS AND RABBI JACQUES CUKIERKORN, BY PERMISSION OF THE UNIVERSITY OF MISSOURI PRESS. COPYRIGHT ©2009 BY THE CURATORS OF THE UNIVERSITY OF MISSOURI.

I was born at the end of the Holocaust and just a few months before the United States dropped two atomic bombs on Japan, marking the start of the nuclear age. Among my contemporaries were such murderers as Adolf Hitler, Josef Stalin, Benito Mussolini, Pol Pot, Idi Amin and Osama bin Laden. So like all Middle Americans who were born in — or lived through — 1945 and what came after it, I have felt required to try to come up with some answer, however tentative, to the ancient mystery that theologians call the question of theodicy: Why is there evil in the world if God is good?

What those of us who have tried out various answers to that question have learned is that all theodicies fail. In the end, there is no exhaustive explanation of suffering and evil. All those of us who are Christian know about it is that, in the end, God intends to redeem the whole creation and put things to right. We can say God is testing us. We can blame it on human weakness and sin. We can blame Satan. Or we can concoct a hybrid answer that mixes and matches those and countless other attempts. And when we get done we still must acknowledge that our answers can't explain evil in all its raw, debilitating, destructive, awesome reality.

That acknowledgment is humbling. But still more humbling is the realization that we ourselves — we Middle Americans who often think of ourselves as the good guys, the people with the good hearts, the decent people — are part of the problem. To be sure, we are, individually and collectively, capable of enormous good. And often we have performed that good by feeding the hungry, housing the homeless, liberating the captive, comforting the afflicted, afflicting the comfortable and using our prophetic voices to call others to act on behalf of what is good, decent, noble and uplifting. We have done what Jews are called to do with their phrase *tikkun olam* — repair the world.

But we also have lived selfishly, lived in ways that wound the Earth, ways that perpetuate economic, social, sexual and racial injustice. We often have wasted one of the most precious gifts we have — time — on mindless pursuits that offer neither needed relaxation nor important moral advancement. We have spent our spare time gambling, watching tedious television shows with odious values, playing violent video games, destroying forests and meadows so we can ride expensive vehicles that pollute the air and chew up the land. We are, in short, a community of screw-ups.

The list of the ways we have contributed to evil in the world is embarrassingly long, and, in the end, we would do well to worry about what's on that list rather than about causes for evil beyond ourselves. Hannah Arendt, who wrote about the Adolf Eichmann trial in Jerusalem[32], put a name to much of this: the banality of evil. It was a way of acknowledging that even the most ordinary of us is capable of the kind of horrific malevolence that has marked our era on this planet. (Some Middle Americans would put all abortions on that list of evil; others of us, by contrast, think life is more complicated than that, though we find the number of abortions in the United States distressing and at times unconscionable.)

In my last book, my co-author and I wrote about the unspeakable evil of the Holocaust and of the brave few who risked their own lives to save Jews in Poland. If I came away from the experience of writing *They Were Just People: Stories of Rescue in Poland During the Holocaust* with a conclusion I did not anticipate when the work began, it had to do not with the banality of evil but with the banality of goodness. By which I mean this: simple, everyday people are capable of performing heroic acts — including ones that save lives. And they are capable of imagining that what they did was not out of the ordinary.

Once when my coauthor, Rabbi Jacques Cukierkorn, and I were in Gdansk, Poland, we interviewed a man who, as an adolescent, was part of a family that saved Jews. It took a lot of back and forth for us to arrange the interview with him. But not long into it we both realized that he was a supreme pain in the ass for reasons unimportant to my current point, and we didn't use his story in our book. That night, as Jacques and I were on a plane, he turned to me and said he thought that was the best interview we would ever do for our book. I looked at him as if it had lost his mind. No, no, he said. Look: If such a jerk could perform risky acts of courage to save lives, everyone is capable of such good deeds. Then, with a little chuckle, Jacques added in his Brazilian Portuguese accent, "even a Presbyterian like you."

It is easy for every generation to imagine that the era in which it lives is unique in human history, that each era has seen the greatest inventions, the greatest statesmen, the greatest evil and on and on. And people who have studied history even a little ought to be reluctant to engage in that kind of exceptionalism. But it is true that the era that began in 1945 was the first in which it was possible for humanity essentially to destroy the world in a flash, making Earth unlivable. The fact that so far we have managed not to do that — at least not in one quick blow — must be counted among our credits. But the fact that we have failed to remove from our hands the instruments that would make such destruction possible must be counted against us.

Middle Americans have long lived under the shadow of this potential destruction. It has followed us like a threatening storm cloud. It has filled the crevices of our minds like smoke. Everything we have done has been done with the understanding that life is contingent, fragile, temporary. We know, because of the Holocaust, that even without nuclear weapons humanity is capable of genocide. And we know, because of Hiroshima and Nagasaki, that we are willing to unleash the most powerful forces of nature on other human beings. (I'm not arguing that Harry S. Truman was wrong to drop the bomb, at least the first one. In the devilish economy of war, I suspect that I and most other Middle Americans would have made the same decision to save American lives at the cost of Japanese lives.)

So when future generations analyze how we Middle Americans did, it will be important for them to remember the context in which we lived, a context that for the first time in human history meant that our minds and, indeed, our hearts never forgot that the world could end tomorrow — and that humanity itself could cause that end to come.

That does not excuse our mistakes, our miscalculations, our sins, our own evil. But it does mean that among all the rest of what we had to face in life, we were the first to have to stare at the immensity of our own destructive power. A realization of that scope "wakes all the waves, all their loose, wandering fire," wrote Theodore Roethke in his book of poems, *The Far Field*.[34]

And what an awesome responsibility it has been to live with that knowledge and not let destruction come to full, vile, evil flower. And what a joy it has been to do at least some good despite our own potential to contribute to that evil.

[1]   *Kurt Vonnegut Letters*, edited by Dan Wakefield, Delacorte Press, 2012, page 259

[2]   "Chicago Is the Future," an "Easy Chair" essay by Thomas Frank, *Harper's Magazine*, December 2013, page 7

[3]   Quoted in *Missouri School Journal*, Volume 39, 1922, page 110. See: http://bit.ly/19ZDwqF.

[4]   *Psychological Types*, by Carl Gustav Jung, 1923 edition, page 82, chapter 1, quoted in *Bartlett's Familiar Quotations*, by John Bartlett, Seventeenth Edition, Little, Brown and Company, 2002, page 675

5   *Lord of the Flies*, by William Golding, Perigee Books, 1959

6   *True Believer: Thoughts on the Nature of Mass Movements*, by Eric Hoffer; Harper Perennial Modern Classics, 2010

7   Op. Cit., *Kurt Vonnegut Letters*, pages 86-87

8   http://boomkids.com

9   *Religious Literacy: What Every American Needs to Know – And Doesn't*, by Stephen Prothero, page 6, HarperSanFrancisco, 2007

10 *The Global Public Square: Religious Freedom and the Making of a World Safe for Diversity*, by Os Guinness, page 54, Intervarsity Press, 2013

11 *Blessed: A History of the American Prosperity Gospel*, by Kate Bowler, Oxford University Press, 2013, Page 233

12 See *Almost Christian: What the Faith of Our Teenagers Is Telling the American Church*, by Kenda Creasy Dean, Oxford University Press, 2010

13 The book to read is *Accompany Them with Singing: The Christian Funeral*, by Thomas G. Long, Westminster John Knox Press, 2009

14 *Future Shock*, by Alvin Toffler, Random House, 1970

15 *Of Human Bondage*, by W. Somerset Maugham, Wilder Publications, 2010, Page 193

16 The book to read is *What Do We Tell the Children?: Talking to Kids about Death and Dying*, by Joseph M. Primo, Abingdon Press, 2013

17 1950 population of Woodstock from U.S. Census Bureau. See 23761117v1ch05.zip at http://www.census.gov/prod/www/decennial.html under Vol. I. Number of Inhabitants, then Vol. I. Number of Inhabitants. * - Title Page [PDF], Full Document [ZIP, 250.4 MB]

18 The book to read is *Unapologetic*, by Francis Spufford, Harper One, 2013

19 See: http://bit.ly/17oDKUv

20 See: http://www.iata.org/pressroom/pr/pages/2012-12-06-01.aspx

21 See: http://www.transtats.bts.gov/Data_Elements.aspx?Data=1

22 *Bowling Alone: The Collapse and Revival of American Community*, by Robert D. Putnam, Touchstone Books by Simon & Schuster, 2001

23 *Lincoln and His World, Volume Three, The Rise to National Prominence, 1843-1853*, by Richard Lawrence Miller, McFarland & Company, Inc., Publishers; page 328

24 Ibid. page 328

25 The book to read is *What's the Matter with Kansas?: How Conservatives Won the Heart of America*, by Thomas Frank, Holt Paperbacks, 2005

26 See: http://www.ssa.gov/pressoffice/basicfact.htm

27 See: http://www.potw.org/archive/potw351.html

28 The documentary to watch is "The Fog of War." See: http://www.sonyclassics.com/fogofwar/

29 See: http://www.hks.harvard.edu/pepg/PDF/Papers/PEPG12-03_CatchingUp.pdf

30 The book to read is Volume Two of *Lincoln and His World: Prairie Politician, 1834-1842*, by Richard Lawrence Miller, Stackpole Books, 2008

31 You can search for names on the wall at this site: http://thewall-usa.com/

32 *Eichmann in Jerusalem: A Report on the Banality of Evil*, by Hannah Arendt, Penguin Classics, 2006

33 *They Were Just People: Stories of Rescue in Poland During the Holocaust*, by Bill Tammeus and Rabbi Jacques Cukierkorn, University of Missouri Press, 2009

34 *The Far Field*, by Theodore Roethke, Doubleday & Co., 1998

CPSIA information can be obtained at www.ICGtesting.com
Printed in the USA
LVOW01s0530300914

406511LV00004B/18/P

9 781491 856024